Red Ribbon
on a
White Horse

OTHER BOOKS BY ANZIA YEZIERSKA

Bread Givers

How I Found America: Collected Stories of Anzia Yezierska

The Open Cage: An Anzia Yezierska Collection

My Story
ANZIA YEZIERSKA

RED RIBBON
on a
WHITE HORSE

Introduction by W. D. Auden
Afterword by Louise Levitas Henriksen

A Karen and Michael Braziller Book
PERSEA BOOKS / NEW YORK

To my daughter Louise Levitas

"Poverty becomes a wise man
like a ribbon on a white horse."

—GHETTO PROVERB

For information, contact the publisher:
PERSEA BOOKS
*853 Broadway
New York, N.Y. 10003*

*First published in 1950 by Charles Scribner's Sons.
First Persea edition, 1981. Revised edition published in 1987.*

*Library of Congress Cataloging-in-Publication Data
Yezierska, Anzia, 1885-
Red ribbon on a white horse.*

I. Title
PS3547.E95R43   1987   813'.52   87-7878
ISBN 0-89255-124-0(pbk.)

Manufactured in the United States of America

CONTENTS

PART THREE

INTRODUCTION

BY W. H. AUDEN

Reading Miss Yezierska's book sets me thinking again about that famous and curious statement in the Preamble to the Constitution about the self-evident right of all men to "the pursuit of happiness," for I have read few accounts of such a pursuit as truthful and moving as hers.

To be happy means to be free, not from pain or fear, but from care or anxiety. A man is so free when (1) he knows what he desires and (2) what he desires is real and not fantastic. A desire is real when the possibility of satisfaction exists for the individual who entertains it and the existence of such a possibility depends, first, on his present historical and social situation—a desire for a Cadillac which may be real for a prosperous American businessman would be fantastic for a Chinese peasant—and, secondly, on his natural endowment as an individual—for a girl with one eye to desire to be kept by a millionaire would be fantastic, for a girl with two beautiful ones it may not. To say that the satisfaction of a desire is possible does not mean that it is certain but that if the desire is not satisfied, a definite and meaningful reason can be given. Thus if the American businessman fails to get the Cadillac he desires and asks himself, "Why?" he has a sensible answer, say: "My wife had to have an emergency operation which took my savings"; but if the Chinese peasant asks, "Why cannot I buy a Cadillac?" there are an infinite number of reasons which can only be summed up in the quite irrational answer, "Because I am I." The businessman suffers disappointment or pain but

11

does not become unhappy; the peasant, unless he dismisses his desire as fantastic, becomes unhappy because to question his lack of satisfaction is to question the value of his existence.

So long as it is a matter of immediate material goods, few sane individuals cherish fantastic desires after the age of puberty, but there are desires for spiritual goods which are much more treacherous, e.g., the desire to find a vocation in life, to have a dedicated history. "What do I want to be? A writer? A chemist? A priest?" Since I am concerned not with any immediate objective good but with pledging the whole of my unknown future in advance, the chances of self-deception are much greater because it will be years before I can be certain whether my choice is real or fantastic. Nor can any outsider make the decision for me; he can only put questions to me which make me more aware of what my decision involves.

Miss Yezierska's book is an account of her efforts to discard fantastic desires and find real ones, both material and spiritual.

She began life in a Polish ghetto, i.e., in the bottom layer of the stratified European heap. In the more advanced countries of Europe, like England, it had become possible for a talented individual to rise a class, a generation, but in Russia, above all for a Jew, it was still quite impossible; if once one had been born in the ghetto, then in the ghetto one would die. For its inhabitants extreme poverty and constant fear of a pogrom were normal, and even so humble a desire as the wish to eat white bread was fantastic. So it had been for centuries until, suddenly, a possibility of escape was opened—immigration to America. What America would provide positively in place of the ghetto remained to be seen, but at least it would be different and any sufferings she might inflict would, at the very least, not be worse.

So Miss Yezierska and her family came and found themselves on the Lower East Side. Here was poverty still but less absolute, exploitation but the possibility of

one day becoming an exploiter, racial discrimination but
no pogroms. Was their new condition an improvement
on their former one? It was hard to be certain. Where
poverty is accepted as normal and permanent, the poor
develop a certain style of living which extracts the max-
imum comfort from the minimum materials, but where
poverty is held to be temporary or accidental, the pre-
occupation with escape leaves no time for such amenities;
every European visitor to the States, I think, receives the
impression that nowhere else in the world is real poverty
—admittedly, rarer here than anywhere else—so cheerless,
sordid, and destitute of all grace.

Moreover, in the "bad old days" of which Miss Yezierska writes—a more lively social conscience and a slack-
ening of the immigrant stream have largely put a stop
to it—in no European country, it seems, were the very
poor treated with such a total disregard of their human
rights. In Europe the rich man and the poor man were
thought of as being two different kinds of men; the poor
man might be an inferior kind but he was a man: but
here the poor man was not, as such, a man, but a person
in a state of poverty from which, if he were a real man,
he would presently extricate himself. The newly arriv-
ing poor, to judge from Miss Yezierska's description of
the sweatshop, were treated by their predecessors, it
seems, like freshmen by upperclassmen, i.e., subjected to
a process of "hazing" so as to toughen their character and
stiffen their determination to rise to a position of immunity.

For the older generation particularly, who, in any case,
had usually immigrated for the sake of their children, not
of themselves, the new life often seemed only a little
better materially, and spiritually very much worse. The
fellowship of suffering lasts only so long as none of the
sufferers can escape. Open a door through which many
but probably not all can escape one at a time and the
neighborly community may disintegrate, all too easily,
into a stampeding crowd. Those who had learned how

to be happy even in prison and could neither understand nor desire another life stood abandoned, watching the stampede with bewilderment and horror.

Some, like Boruch Shlomoi Mayer, simply wanted to go back:

> To me, America is a worse *Goluth* than Poland. The ukases and pogroms from the Czar, all the killings that could not kill us gave us the strength to live with God. Learning was learning—dearer than gold. . . . But here in New York, the synagogues are in the hands of godless lumps of flesh. A butcher, a grocer, any money-maker could buy himself into a president of a synagogue. With all that was bad under the Czar, the synagogue was still God's light in time of darkness. Better to die there than to live here. . . .

Others continued to live their old life with uncompromising indifference to the new world. Miss Yezierska's father, for instance, had a vocation, the study of the Torah, which involved his being supported by his wife and children. He had expected them to do so in Plinsk, he expected them to continue doing so in New York. But what they had accepted in Poland as an extra burden, worth bearing for the honor in which a learned and holy man was held by the community, was bound to seem intolerable in America, where not only was a non-earner regarded as an idler but also the possibility for the family of acquiring status existed in proportion to their earning capacity.

His daughter, however, as she later realized, was more like him than either of them at the time could perceive. Had she been less like him, had she simply desired money and a good marriage, there would have been less friction between them but she, too, was seeking for a dedicated life of her own, which in his eyes was impious, for all vocations but one were for men only.

"A woman alone, not a wife and not a mother, has no existence." She, however, wanted a vocation all to herself and thought she had found it in writing. She began, as she tells us, with the hope that "by writing out what I don't know and can't understand, it would stop hurting me." At the same time, of course, she wanted money to satisfy her needs. This is any artist's eternal problem, that he needs money as a man but works for love. Even in the case of the most popular writer, money is not the purpose for which he writes, though popularity may be.

So she begins; she writes a book *Hungry Hearts* about the life of a poor immigrant, which is well reviewed but does not sell; then, suddenly, the American Fairy— whether she is a good or a wicked fairy, who knows?— waves her wand and she is transported in an instant from Hester Street to Hollywood; from one day to the next, that is, suffering is abolished for her. How does she feel? More unhappy than she has ever been in her life. To have the desires of the poor and be transferred in a twinkling of an eye to a world which can only be real for those who have the desires of the rich is to be plunged into the severest anxiety. The foreshortening of time which is proper to a dream or a fairy story is a nightmare in actual life.

Further, to be called to Hollywood is not like winning a fortune in the Calcutta sweepstake; money is showered upon one because it is believed that one is a valuable piece of property out of which much larger sums can be made. For a writer this is only bearable if he knows exactly what he wants to write and if what he can write happens to pay off the investors as they expect. Miss Yezierska was too young to be the former and, by snatching her away from Hester Street and the only experiences about which she knew, the film magnates effectively destroyed the possibility that their expensive goose might lay another golden egg. In fact, they gave it such a fright that it stopped laying altogether.

The sudden paralysis or drying up of the creative power occurs to artists everywhere but nowhere, perhaps, more frequently than in America; nowhere else are there so many writers who produced one or two books in their youth and then nothing. I think the reason for this is the dominance of the competitive spirit in the American ethos. A material good like a washing machine is not a unique good but one example of a kind of good; accordingly one washing machine can be compared with another and judged better or worse. The best, indeed the only, way to stimulate the production of better washing machines is by competition. But a work of art is not a good of a certain kind but a unique good so that, strictly speaking, no work of art is comparable to another. An inferior washing machine is preferable to no washing machine at all, but a work of art is either acceptable, whatever its faults, to the individual who encounters it or unacceptable, whatever its merits. The writer who allows himself to become infected by the competitive spirit proper to the production of material goods so that, instead of trying to write *his* book, he tries to write one which is better than somebody else's book is in danger, because of the unreality of such an attempt, of trying to write the absolute masterpiece which will eliminate all competition once and for all and, since this task is totally unreal, his creative powers cannot relate to it, and the result is sterility.

In other and more static societies than in the United States an individual derives much of his sense of identity and value from his life-membership in a class—the particular class is not important—from which neither success nor failure, unless very spectacular, can oust him, but, in a society where any status is temporary and any variation in the individual's achievement alters it, his sense of his personal value must depend—unless he is a religious man—largely upon what he achieves: the more successful he is, the nearer he comes to the ideal good of absolute certainty as to his value; the less successful he is, the nearer he comes to the abyss of nonentity.

With the coming of the depression Miss Yezierska

ceased to be a solitary failure and became one of millions who could not be called failures, because the positions in which they could succeed or fail no longer existed. It was surely the height of irony that in a country where the proof of one's importance had been that one was rich and popular, people should suddenly, in order to prove that they were important enough to eat, have to go to elaborate lengths to establish that they were penniless and friendless.

The Arts Project of W.P.A. was, perhaps, one of the noblest and most absurd undertakings ever attempted by any state. Noblest because no other state has ever cared whether its artists as a group lived or died; other governments have hired certain individual artists to glorify their operations and have even granted a small pension from time to time to some artist with fame or influence, but to consider, in a time of general distress, starving artists as artists and not simply as paupers is unique to the Roosevelt Administration. Yet absurd, because a state can only function bureaucratically and impersonally—it has to assume that every member of a class is equivalent or comparable to every other member—but every artist, good or bad, is a member of a class of one. You can collect fifty unemployed plumbers, test them to eliminate the unemployable, and set the remainder to work on whatever plumbing jobs you can find, but if you collect fifty unemployed writers, ex-professors, New England spinsters, radicals, bohemians, etc., there is no test of their abilities which applies fairly to them all and no literary task you can devise which can be properly done by even a minority of them. While only the laziest and most inefficient of your plumbers will let you down, because the jobs you give them are the jobs for which they have been trained and regard as theirs, only the writers with the strictest sense of moral, as distinct from professional, duty will fail to cheat you if, as must almost inevitably be the case, the literary job you offer them is one in which they take no interest, not because writers are intrinsically lazier or more dishonest than plumbers, but because they can see no sense in what you ask them to do.

It is easy for the accountant to frown on W.P.A. for its inefficiency and for the artists to sneer at it for its bureaucracy, but the fact remains that, thanks to it, a number of young artists of talent were enabled, at a very critical time in their lives, to get started on their creative careers. As for the rest, the executive might just as well —and I dare say would have been glad to—have been honest, given them their weekly checks and sent them home, but the legislature which could endure such honesty could exist only in heaven.

Among her companions in poverty and comedy, Miss Yezierska felt once more to some degree that happiness of "belonging" which years before she had felt in Hester Street, though she realized it only after she had left. But belonging to some degree is not enough; one must belong completely or the feeling soon withers. Once again the lack of a common memory of the past and a common anticipation of the future was a fatal barrier, not only for her but for most of her fellows.

> The word "home" raised a smile in us all three,
> And one repeated it, smiling just so
> That all knew what he meant and none would say.
> Between three counties far apart that lay
> We were divided and looked strangely each
> At the other, and we knew we were not friends
> But fellows in a union that ends
> With the necessity for it, as it ought.

No, the accidental community of suffering was not the clue to happiness and she must look further; where she went and what she found the reader can learn for himself.

Miss Yezierska's autobiography is, literally, the story

of an early twentieth-century immigrant, but it has a deeper and more general significance today when, figuratively, the immigrant is coming more and more to stand as the symbol for Everyman, for the natural and unconscious community of tradition is rapidly disappearing from the earth.

Red Ribbon
on a
White Horse

"Not in the flesh, not in the spirit even,
Not in the cunning of the brain that rides
In mastery upon the roads of heaven,

Or charts the rhythm of the starry tides,
The answer and the truth are found, but where,
Deep at the very core, the Stranger bides—"

JOHN HALL WHEELOCK

PART ONE

~~~~~~

CHAPTER I

HESTER STREET

I PAUSED in front of my rooming house on Hester Street. This was 1920, when Hester Street was the push-cart center of the East Side. The air reeked with the smell of fish and overripe fruit from the carts in front of the house. I peeked into the basement window. The landlady was not there to nag me for the rent. I crept into her kitchen, filled my pitcher with water and hurried out. In my room I set the kettle boiling. There wasn't much taste to the stale tea leaves but the hot water warmed me. I was still sipping my tea, thankful for this short reprieve from my landlady, when I heard my name shouted outside the door.

The angel of death, I thought, my landlady had come to put me out! And Hester Street had gathered to watch another eviction. I opened the door with fear.

Mrs. Katz with her baby in her arms, Mrs. Rubin drying her wet hands on her apron, and Zalmon Shlomoh, the fish peddler, crowded into my room, pushing forward a Western Union messenger who handed me a yellow envelope.

"*Oi-oi weh!* A telegram!" Mrs. Rubin wailed. "Somebody died?"

Their eyes gleamed with prying curiosity. "Read—read already!" they clamored.

I ripped open the envelope and read:

TELEPHONE IMMEDIATELY FOR AN APPOINTMENT
TO DISCUSS MOTION PICTURE RIGHTS OF "HUNGRY
HEARTS"

R. L. GIFFEN

"Who died?" they demanded.

"Nobody died. It's only a place for a job," I said, shoo-
ing them out of the room.

I reread the message. "Telephone immediately!" It
was from one of the big moving-picture agents. In those
days Hollywood was still busy with Westerns and Pollyanna romances. The studios seldom bought stories from
life. This was like winning a ticket on a lottery.

Hungry Hearts had been my first book. It had been
praised by the critics, esteemed as literature. That meant
it didn't sell. After spending the two hundred dollars I
had received in royalties, I was even poorer than when
I had started writing.

And now movie rights! Money! Wealth! I could get
the world for the price of a telephone call. But if I had
had a nickel for a telephone I wouldn't have fooled a
starving stomach with stewed-over tea leaves. I needed
a nickel for telephoning, ten cents for carfare—fifteen
cents! What could I pawn to get fifteen cents?

I looked about my room. The rickety cot didn't belong
to me. The rusty gas plate on the window sill? My typewriter? The trunk that was my table? Then I saw the
shawl, my mother's shawl that served as a blanket and
a cover for my cot.

Nobody in our village in Poland had had a shawl like
it. It had been Mother's wedding present from her rich
uncle in Warsaw. It had been her Sabbath, her holiday.
. . . When she put it on she outshone all the other
women on the way to the synagogue.

Old and worn—it held memories of my childhood, put
space and color in my drab little room. It redeemed the
squalor in which I had to live. But this might be the last

time I'd have to pawn it. I seized the shawl and rushed with it to the pawnshop.

Zaretsky, the pawnbroker, was a bald-headed dwarf, grown gray with the years in the dark basement—tight-skinned and crooked from squeezing pennies out of despairing people.

I watched his dirty, bony fingers appraise the shawl. "An old rag!" he grunted, peering at me through his thick-rimmed glasses. He had always intimidated me before, but this time the telegram in my hand made me bold.

"See here, Zaretzky," I said, "this shawl is rarer than diamonds—an antique from Poland, pure wool. The older it gets, the finer—the softer the colors——"

He spread it out and held it up to the light. "A moth-eaten rag full of holes!"

"You talk as if I were a new customer. You make nothing of the best things. As you did with my samovar."

"A samovar is yet something. But this!" He pushed the shawl from him. "A quarter. Take it or leave it."

"This was the finest shawl in Plinsk. It's hand-woven, hand-dyed. People's lives are woven into it."

"For what is past nobody pays. Now it's junk—falling apart."

"I'm only asking a dollar. It's worth ten times that much. Only a dollar!"

"A quarter. You want it? Yes or no?"

I grabbed the quarter and fled.

Within a half-hour I was at the agent's office.

"I've great news for you," he said, drawing up a chair near his desk. "I've practically sold your book to Hollywood. Goldwyn wants it. Fox is making offers, too, but I think Goldwyn is our best bet. They offered five thousand dollars. I'm holding out for ten."

I had pawned Mother's shawl to get there, and this man talked of thousands of dollars. Five, ten thousand dollars was a fortune in 1920. I was suddenly aware of my hunger. I saw myself biting into thick, juicy steaks, dipping fresh rolls into mounds of butter, swallowing whole platters of French fried potatoes in one gulp.

"If we settle with Goldwyn," Mr. Giffen said, "he will want you to go to Hollywood to collaborate on the script."

I stood up to go, dizzy from lack of food and so much excitement.

"Maybe what you're saying is real," I said. "If it is, then can you advance me one dollar on all these thousands?"

Smiling, he handed me a bill.

I walked out of his office staring at the ten-dollar bill in my hand. Directly across the street was the white-tiled front of a Child's restaurant. How often I had stood outside this same restaurant, watching the waitresses clear away leftover food and wanting to cry out, "Don't throw it away! Give it to me. I'm hungry!" I stumbled through the door, sank into the first vacant chair and ordered the most expensive steak on the menu. A platter was set before me—porterhouse steak, onions, potatoes, rolls, butter. I couldn't eat fast enough. Before I was half through, my throat tightened. My head bent over my plate, tears rolled down my cheeks onto the uneaten food.

When I hadn't had a penny for a roll I had had the appetite of a wolf that could devour the earth. Now that I could treat myself to a dollar dinner, I couldn't take another bite. But just having something to eat, even though I could only half eat it, made me see the world with new eyes. If only Father and Mother were alive now! How I longed to be at peace with them!

I had not meant to abandon them when I left home— I had only wanted to get to the place where I belonged. To do it, I had to strike out alone.

If my mother could only have lived long enough to see that I was not the heartless creature I seemed to be! As for my father—would he forgive me even now?

Now that there was no longer reason to feel sorry for myself, my self-pity turned to regret for all that I did not do and might have done for them.

The waitress started to remove the dishes.

"I'm not through!" I held onto the plate, still starved for the steak and potatoes I could not eat. The agent's talk of Hollywood might have been only a dream. But steak was real. When no one was looking, I took out my handkerchief, thrust the meat and cold potatoes into it, covered it with my newspaper and sneaked out like a thief with the food for which I had paid.

Back in my room I opened the newspaper bundle, still too excited with the prospect of Hollywood to be able to eat. "God! What a hoarding creature I've become!" I cried out in self-disgust. In my purse was the change from the ten-dollar bill the agent had given me. More than enough for a dozen meals. And yet the hoarding habit of poverty was so deep in my bones that I had to bring home the food that I could not eat.

I leaned out of the window. Lily, the alley cat, was scavenging the garbage can as usual. I had named her Lily because she had nothing but garbage to eat and yet somehow looked white and beautiful like the lilies that rise out of dunghills.

"Lily!" I called to her, holding up the steak. The next moment she bounded up on my window sill, devouring the steak and potatoes in huge gulps.

"I've been a pauper all my life," I told Lily as I watched her eat. "But I'll be a pauper no longer. I'll have money, plenty of it. I'll not only have money to buy food when I'm hungry, but I'll have men who'll love me on my terms. An end to hoarding food, or hoarding love!"

I threw open the trunk, dug down and yanked out the box of John Morrow's letters, determined to tear them up and shed the memory of them once and for all. For years those letters had been to me music and poetry. I had stayed up nights to console my loneliness reading and rereading them, drugged with the opiate of his words.

But now, with the prospect of Hollywood, I began to hate those letters. Why hang on to words when the love that had inspired them was dead? In Hollywood there would be new people. There would be other men.

I seized the first letter and began tearing it. But a panicky fear of loss stopped me. Money could buy meat and mink, rye bread and rubies, but not the beauty of his words. Those letters were my assurance that I was a woman who could love and be loved. Without them, I was again the oddity of Hester Street, an object of pity and laughter.

"Poor thing! I can't stand the starved-dog look in her eyes," I had overheard one of the men in the shop say to another.

"Well, if you're so sorry for her, marry her," came the jeering retort.

"Marry her? Oi-i-i! Oi-yoi! That *meshugeneh?* That redheaded witch? Her head is on wheels, riding on air. She's not a woman. She has a *dybbuk,* a devil, a book for a heart."

But when I met John Morrow, the *dybbuk* that drove away other men had drawn him to me. He saw my people in me, struggling for a voice. I could no more tear up those letters than I could root out the memory of him!

I slipped the torn pieces of the letter into the envelope, put it back with the others in the box and stuck it at the bottom of my trunk, under my old clothes.

A week later Mr. Giffen asked me to lunch to talk over the movie contract I was to sign.

After I had signed a twenty-page contract, Giffen handed me a check—a check made out to me—a check for nine thousand dollars.

"I've deducted one thousand for my ten per cent," he explained.

I looked at the check. Nine thousand dollars!

"Riches for a lifetime!" I cried.

Giffen smiled. "It's only the beginning. When you're in Hollywood you'll see the more you have, the more you'll get."

He took out my railroad reservation from his wallet and handed it to me. "They want you to assist in the production of the book. You're to get two hundred a week and all your expenses while there."

He gave me another check for a hundred dollars. "This is for your incidentals on the train. Meals for three and a half days—one hundred dollars. Not so bad!" He patted my hand. "Young lady! You go on salary the moment you step on the train."

I told him I could be ready as soon as I got something out of a pawnshop.

With my purse full of money, I hurried to Zaretzky's to redeem my shawl.

"Zaretzky!" I charged into the basement. "I forgot to take my receipt for the shawl!"

"Forgot, nothing! I gave it to you in your hand."

"I swear to you, I left it on the counter."

"If you were crazy enough to lose it, it's not my fault."

I took out a five-dollar bill. "Here's five dollars for your quarter," I said. "What more do you want?"

He made no move. He stood like stone staring at me.

"Shylock! Here's ten dollars! I have no time to bargain with you. If that's not enough, here's twice ten dollars! Twenty dollars for your twenty-five cents!"

There was a flicker in the black pinpoints of his eyes. He took out a signed receipt from the money box. "I sold it the day you brought it here for five dollars," he groaned, his face distorted by frustrated greed.

The next day I packed my belongings without the shawl that had gone with me everywhere I went. The loss of that one beautiful thing which all my money could not reclaim shadowed my prospective trip to Hollywood.

The distrust of good fortune always in the marrow of my bones made me think of my father. While I was struggling with hunger and want, trying to write, I feared to go near him. I couldn't stand his condemnation of my lawless, godless, selfish existence. But now, with Hollywood ahead of me, I had the courage to face him. As I entered the dark hallway of the tenement where he lived, I heard his voice chanting.

"And a man shall be as a hiding place from the wind, and covert from the tempest; as rivers of water in a dry place, as the shadow of a great rock in a weary land . . ."

Since earliest childhood I had heard this chant of Isaiah. It was as familiar to me as Mother Goose rhymes to other children. Hearing it again after so many years, I was struck for the first time by the beauty of the words. Though my father was poor and had nothing, the Torah, the poetry of prophets, was his daily bread.

He was still chanting as I entered, a gray-bearded man in a black skullcap.

"And the eyes of them that see shall not be dim, and the ears of them that hear shall hearken. The heart of the rash shall understand knowledge, and the tongue of the stammerers shall be ready to speak plainly . . ."

As I stood there, waiting for him to see me, I noticed the aging stoop of his shoulders. He was getting paler, thinner. The frail body accused me for having been away so long. But in the same moment of guilt the smells of the musty room in which he wouldn't permit a window to be opened or a book to be dusted made me want to run. On the table piled high with his papers and dust-laden books were dishes with remains of his last meal—cabbage soup and pumpernickel. He was as unaware of the squalor around him as a medieval monk.

Dimly I realized that this new world didn't want his kind. He had no choice but to live for God. And I, his daughter, who abandoned him for the things of this world, had joined the world against him.

He looked up and saw me.

"So you've come at last? You've come to see your old father?"

"I was so busy. . . ." I mumbled. And then, hastily, to halt his reproaches, I reached into my bag and dropped ten ten-dollar bills on the open page of his book. He pushed aside the bills as if they would contaminate the holiness of the script.

"Months, almost a year, you've been away. . . ."

"Bessie, Fannie live right near here, they promised to look after you. . . ."

"They have their own husbands to look after. You're my only unmarried daughter. Your first duty to God is to serve your father. But what's an old father to an *Amerikanerin,* a daughter of Babylon?"

"Your daughter of Babylon brought you a hundred dollars."

"Can your money make up for your duty as a daughter? In America, money takes the place of God."

"But I earned that money with my writing." For all his scorn of my godlessness, I thought he would take a father's pride in my success. "Ten thousand they paid me. . . ."

He wouldn't let me finish. He shook a warning finger in my face. "Can you touch pitch without being defiled? Neither can you hold on to all that money without losing your soul."

Even in the street, his words still rang in my ears. "Daughter of Babylon! You've polluted your inheritance. . . . You'll wander in darkness and none shall be there to save you. . . ."

His old God could not save me in a new world, I told myself. Why did we come to America, if not to achieve all that had been denied us for centuries in Europe? Fear and poverty were behind me. I was going into a new world of plenty. I would learn to live in the now . . . not in the next world.

I had but to open my purse, look at my reservation for a drawing room on the fastest flyer to Hollywood, think of the fabulous salary I was to be paid even while traveling, and no hope in which I might indulge was too high, no longing too visionary.

Grand Central Station, where I waited for my train,

seemed an unreal place. Within the vast marble structure people rushed in and out, meeting, parting and hurrying on, each in pursuit of his own dream. As I stood lost in my thoughts, every man I saw seemed John Morrow coming to see me off. If so incredible a thing could happen as my going to Hollywood, surely John Morrow could appear. He must know *Hungry Hearts* was written for him. He must sense my need to share my wealth with him even more than I had needed him in poverty.

The gates opened. My train was called. I picked up my bundle, started through the gate, still looking back, still expecting the miracle. I could not give up the hope that love as great as his had been could ever cease.

The first days and nights on the train I was too dazed by the sudden turn of events to notice the view from my window. Miles of beautiful country I saw, unaware of what I was seeing. Then one morning I woke up and saw the desert stretching out on both sides. The train raced through the wide monotonous landscape at a terrific pace to reach its destination on scheduled time.

It was getting hotter and hotter. Sand sifted through the screened air vents and closed doors. The train stopped at the station to refuel. Passengers stepped out to buy trinkets from the Indians squatting on the platform. Over the entrance of an adobe building I read in gilt letters the inscription:

THE DESERT WAITED, SILENT AND HOT AND FIERCE IN ITS DESOLATION, HOLDING ITS TREAS-URES UNDER SEAL OF DEATH AGAINST THE COMING OF THE STRONG ONE.

I looked across the vast space and thought of the time when all this silent sand was a rolling ocean. What eons had to pass for the ocean to dry into this arid waste! In the immensity of the desert the whirl of trivialities which I had so magnified all fell away. I was suspended in timelessness—sand, sky, and space. What a relief it

was to let go—not to think—not to feel, but rest, silent
—past, present and future stretching to infinity.

Slowly, imperceptibly, the dry desert air receded before the humid, subtropical warmth of southern California. The sense of time and the concern with self stirred
again. Green hills, dazzling gardens and orange groves,
towering date palms ushered in the great adventure
ahead of me.

~~~~~~

CHAPTER II

TILED BATHROOM OF MY OWN

AT THE Los Angeles station I was met by a man who introduced himself as Mr. Irving Lenz, chief of Goldwyn's publicity department.

"Where's your baggage?" he asked.

I pointed to my bundles. There had been no time to buy luggage or anything else.

In the midst of the crowd coming and going to the trains I found myself surrounded by curious-eyed men and women. Pencils and notebooks were pulled out, cameras opened.

"Who are all these people?" I asked.

"Reporters to interview you," Lenz said.

They stared at me as if I were some strange animal on the way to the zoo.

"To what do you attribute your success?" one of the reporters began.

I looked at him. For days and nights I had been whirled in a Niagara of unreality, wondering what it was all about. And he asked for a formula of success.

"What are you going to do with all your money?" another went on.

While I stood panic-stricken, tongue-tied, cameras clicked, flashlights exploded.

"Take me out of this," I appealed to Mr. Lenz.

"Why, this is part of the game," Lenz laughed. "A million-dollar build-up for your book."

With the cameras still clicking, he took my arm and led me to an automobile.

In one of those limousines which I had always condemned as a criminal luxury, I was driven to the Miramar Hotel. A basket of roses greeted me when I walked into my apartment. No one had ever put flowers in a room for me before. I lifted the roses high in the air, then hugged them to me.

There was a knock at the door. A maid in black and white came in. "Does Madame wish any help in unpacking? Or perhaps in dressing for dinner?"

I was wearing the only clothes I had—blue serge skirt and cotton blouse bought at a basement bargain counter. They were rumpled from travel.

"No, no, I need nothing," I stammered.

With one swift glance she appraised the cheapness and roughness of my clothes and withdrew.

As the door closed behind her, I walked into the bedroom. More flowers. I touched the bed. Clean, soft, smooth. I lifted the bedspread, feasting my eyes on the white sheets, the wool blankets. Who could lie down and disturb this delicate perfection?

Another door. Bathtub, washbowl, and toilet. My own. White-tiled walls. Sunlight streaming in through clean glass windows. Racks with towels—towels big as blankets, bath towels, hand towels. Bath salts in crystal bottles. Soap wrapped in silver foil. Toilet paper, canary-colored to match the towels.

I looked down for the imprint of my shoes on the white-tiled floor. How could I desecrate the cleanliness of that tub with my dirty body? I thought of the hours I had to stand in line at the public bathhouse before Passover and the New Year—and the greasy tub smelling of the sweat of the crowd. The iron sink in the hall on Hester Street. One faucet for eight families. Here were two faucets. Hot water, cold water, all the water in the world. I turned on both faucets and let them run for the sheer joy of it.

I danced across the fawn-colored carpet in the sitting room and flopped down into one easy chair after another. Then up and out to the balcony, down the terrace to the private beach washed by the ocean waves. I looked at the shimmering water dotted with white yachts. The Atlantic led back to Poland. The Pacific stretched to the home of Kublai Khan.

It was too big, too beautiful. Could I ever get used to living in such comfort? Could I enjoy such affluence unless I could forget the poverty back of me? Forget? The real world, the tenement where I had lived, blotted out the sun and sky. I saw myself, a scrawny child of twelve, always hungry, always asking questions. It was soon after we had come to America. We lived on Hester Street in a railroad flat that was always dark. One morning my mother was in the kitchen, bent over the wash-tub, rubbing clothes.

"When was I born?" I asked, pulling her apron. "When is my birthday?"

She gave no sign that she had heard me.

"Minnie, the janitor's daughter, will have a party. A cake with candles on it for a birthday. All children have birthdays. Everybody on the block knows her age but me." I pounded the table with my fist. "I must have a birthday like other children."

"Birthdays?" Mother stopped washing and looked at me, her eyes black with gloom. "A birthday wills itself in you? What is with you the great joy? No shirt on your back—no shoes on your feet—not a penny in the house to buy bread—and you want yet birthdays? The landlord's daughter can have birthdays. For her, the music plays. For her, life is a feast. For you—a funeral. Bury yourself in ashes and weep because you were born in this world."

Like a driven horse feeling the whip behind him, she rubbed the clothes savagely.

"Have you a father like other fathers? Does his wife or his children lay in his head?" Mother wiped the sweat from her face with a heavy hand. "Woe is me! Your father works for God and His Torah like other fathers work for their wives and children. You ought to light a black candle on your birthday. You ought to lie on your face and cry and curse the day you were born!"

The black curse of poverty followed me during my brief, few days in an American school. I had walked into the classroom without knowing a word of English. The teacher was talking to the children. They knew what she was saying and I knew nothing. I felt like the village idiot in my immigrant clothes so different from the clothes of the other children. But more than the difference of appearance was the unfamiliar language. The sound of every foreign word hammered into me: You'll never know, you'll never learn. . . . And before I could learn, poverty thrust me into the sweatshop.

But that was long ago. Now the sun was shining, laughing at my fears. For the first time in my life I had every reason to be happy. I had pushed my way up out of the darkness into light. I had earned my place in the sun. No backward glances! I would shed the very thought of poverty as I had shed my immigrant's shawl. I had learned to abase myself; now I would learn to lift up my head and look the world in the face.

To begin with, I would eat in state in the dining room. I had no clothes for the occasion. But I was too happy to care about my appearance. My shirtwaist and skirt would have to do.

The headwaiter led me to a central table. Music, soft lights, the gleam of silver and glass on snowy linen. Never had I seen such a shimmer of lovely gowns.

I picked up the gilded menu. What a feast! Ten entrées, a dozen roasts, twice as many desserts. Breaking my resolve to forget, I thought of the blocks I used to walk for stale bread to save two cents. The way I bargained at the pushcarts when the Friday rush was over to get the leftover herring a penny cheaper.

And now—choose! Gorge yourself on Terrine de Pâté

de Foie Gras, Green Turtle Soup au Sherry, Jumbo Pigeon on Toast, Canapé Royale Princesse—whatever that is! Choose!

The waiter smiled at me as if he had read my thoughts, and offered me the evening papers. "Your office sent them."

I glanced at the headlines: "Immigrant Wins Fortune in Movies." "Sweatshop Cinderella at the Miramar Hotel." "From Hester Street to Hollywood."

There was a picture of me above those captions, but I couldn't recognize myself in it, any more than I could recognize my own life in the newspapers' stories of my "success."

CHAPTER III

THE PICTURE OF THE CENTURY

"WELL, DUCHESS!" Mr. Lenz rose to greet me as I was shown into his office next morning. "You're the best front-page news since the earthquake."

The gloves in my hands kept twisting around my fingers. The desk, the chair, Mr. Lenz, everything in the room swayed as I tried to find my balance.

In Hester Street I knew my way. Black was black; white was white. Right was right; wrong was wrong. Now black, white, right, wrong—nothing was real any more.

"Those headlines are being rushed through three hundred papers," Lenz went on in his phonographic voice. "With the boost we're giving it, *Hungry Hearts* will be a best seller before we start production."

I had dreamed of recognition for my book. But those flashy headlines had nothing to do with me or my work. I felt like the beggar who drowned in a barrel of cream. I used to like cream. It had made my mouth water to see those tiny thimbles of cream for coffee which I never could afford to buy. But on the train they served me cream in big silver pitchers three times a day. And now cream had lost its flavor.

"Come, let me show you your office," Lenz said. We walked through the hall. I read the names of the great writers of the twenties on the doors: Will Rogers, Rupert Hughes, Alice Duer Miller, Elinor Glyn, Gertrude Atherton, Katharine Newlin Burt. . . . Then I saw my own name!

I stood still, staring at the gilded letters, filled with the same wonder that I had experienced when I saw my first story in print.

"How do you like it?" Lenz asked, throwing open the door.

I looked at the carpet, the wide mahogany desk, the luxurious couch and big blue leather chair. Artificial coal blazing in the fireplace sent a red glow about the room.

My blood pounded in my stomach. I could feel nothing beyond this.

As I sat down on the swivel chair, a porter walked in and handed me a long white gilt-edged box.

"What's this?" I asked.

"Must be flowers for you," Lenz said.

I tried to untie the gold cord with my fumbling fingers, and then thrust it at Mr. Lenz. "Open it quick, please."

He untied the cord, handed me the box and watched me open it. Red roses. Never had I seen such long stems. Bending over to inhale the perfume, I saw the card. "Greetings to *Hungry Hearts!* The picture of the century!" It was signed "Paul Bern."

"Who is Paul Bern?" I asked.

"He's to direct your picture. He'll be in soon."

I spread out my hands on the glass-topped desk. I had written a book. I had earned all this. This office, my name on the door, this desk, these flowers—proof that I was really a writer.

I opened the drawers of the desk. They were full of white and yellow sheets and envelopes of all sizes, a whole box of carbons. Abundance now, and once I had counted every sheet bought in the five-and-ten-cent store. I had used grocery bags, scraps of wrapping paper, and the backs of envelopes. Now I could be a glutton with paper. Write and rewrite each page a thousand times without worrying over the cost.

"All that brand-new paper waiting to be written on," I said.

"Well, let's see what you can do. Give us another hit." Lenz leaned over the desk and pushed a button. A young girl, crisply dressed, came in from an adjoining room.

"Miss Yezierska—your secretary, Miss Young," Lenz said.

She nodded and smiled.

Miss Young's beauty-parlor grooming fitted her youth like the lacquered shine of her pink, pointed fingernails. Lipstick, mascara, faultless wave of blond hair, silk stockings, slender, delicate feet in patent leather.

"Secretary for me?" I blurted. "I thought secretaries were only for men in business."

"In Hollywood, writing is business." Lenz laughed. "Well, I'll let you get to work." He walked out.

Work? How could I work with this dressed-up doll around me? Her eyes were fixed on my shoes. I returned her look, taking in her high heels.

Miss Young's smooth prettiness, her graceful figure, made me aware of the clumsy peasant that I was. Could I ever achieve her elegance if I went to all the beauty experts of Hollywood?

Living up to this office was enough of a strain, but living up to the secretary—what on earth could I do with her? Instead of working, I saw myself waging an invisible fight with a fashion plate.

She brought a chair to my desk and sat down, pad in hand. "Is there anything you want done?" she asked.

"I don't know," I mumbled, intimidated by her low, modulated voice.

"There's no pencil sharpener," Miss Young said, glancing at the dull point of her pencil. "I can get one from the supply clerk." And she was gone.

While I was still wondering how to get rid of her, Miss Young returned. With swift, efficient hands, she screwed the sharpener on the wall and proceeded to sharpen her pencils.

The sight of those sharp pencils beside her white dictation pad was too much for me.

"Miss Young," I said. "Maybe you . . . Perhaps you could . . . Why don't you go home?"

"Shall I put your flowers in water before I go?" she asked.

As she arranged the flowers in the vase, I noticed how her overrouged lips accentuated the thinness and pallor of her face.

"You don't think I'll do?"

There was a hurt in her eyes that all the mascara and shadow could not hide.

"Maybe—tomorrow—if you'll come back . . ."

"Thank you. I hope I can please you."

The worry in her voice made me think it wasn't a picnic to have one's job depend on moods of cranks like me. The unhappiness in the girl's face drew me as much as her mannequin make-up had repelled me. Something more than the faint scent of powder lingered behind her as she walked out, her heels clicking. I smell misery as some people smell out success, I thought.

I turned to my typewriter. It was the only thing without varnish of newness in the room. I touched the keys. It felt like an old friend. Work, if I could only get to work. . . .

"Welcome! Welcome, wonder child!" A sharp-eyed, tailor-made young man rushed into the room and grabbed my hand. "I'm Paul Bern. I wanted to be the first to say hello to you."

"Hello!" I mumbled, staring at him. He had a dark Hester Street face, but slick as a picture on the cover of a movie magazine.

Beside Paul Bern's swank, my secretary's elegance paled to a tawdry five-and-ten-cent-store imitation. He wore a Scotch-tweed jacket, gray flannel trousers, and a pongee shirt open at the neck. Even the flower in his buttonhole seemed especially designed for him.

"I see you got my roses." He smiled ingratiatingly, shaking my hand.

"Thanks." I tried to withdraw my hand, but he pressed it more warmly.

"Thank you for giving us a book that'll blaze a new trail in pictures. You're what I call a natural-born sob sister."

"Do you mean that for a compliment?" I laughed.

"I mean you've dipped your pen in your heart. You've got the stuff that clicks with the crowd—the stuff that'll coin money."

My hand was hot and wet in his tight grasp.

"I'm planning a production that'll knock their eyes out. A million-dollar budget. Think of that, little one!" A million-dollar budget was tops in 1920.

I wondered when he would release my hand. I wanted to sit down. I didn't know what to do.

"I sweated blood to make Goldwyn buy your story," he went on. "What didn't I go through with that man to make him see the light! But, by God, I put you over, darling!"

"May I come in?" Another, quieter voice interrupted Bern's avalanche of words. Bern dropped my hand. I looked up and saw a tall, thin, sandy-haired young man, his shoulders too broad for his frail body. Bern introduced me to Julian Josephson, the scenario writer.

A strange pair of opposites, I thought, as they drew up their chairs close to my desk. If Julian Josephson had a mirror, he probably never used it. A button was missing from his vest. His pants bagged at the knees. He didn't know, he didn't care how he looked or what he wore. But even the bald spot on his head somehow belonged with his big-boned homely features. It was comforting to look at him and feel him in the room.

He humped over, smoking leisurely, a contrast to the restless Bern, who did all the talking.

"Baby! You should have seen me comb Hollywood to line up our cast." Bern's hand lighted on my shoulder. "I got Schwartz from the Jewish Art Theatre to send us his star for the mother. I held up the shooting date of our picture to get Helen Ferguson for the lead. No one else can do Sara the way it's got to be done. She'll be terrific."

Josephson sat back, his silent gaze following the smoke of his cigarette. From time to time he turned from Bern to me, a glint of amusement in his eyes.

"My dear," Bern went on, smoothing my shoulder, his voice giving honey, "we're all hitching our wagon to your star. This one picture will make a mint of money for us all. You'll see . . ."

The telephone rang. I picked up the receiver. It was for Bern.

He took the call, and then stood up, tall with pride. "Sorry, Goldwyn is waiting for me. But I'll be back. Don't forget, sweet child, we're going to do big things together!"

At the door he kissed his finger tips with the gallantry of a drummer putting over a sale.

"Did you know Goldwyn bought *Hungry Hearts* on his say-so?" Josephson said as the door closed. "That's how much he thinks of him."

I kept silent.

"He comes from your own alley," Josephson went on. "You feel in him something of yourself. . . ."

"No!" I said. "We have nothing in common."

"You have one thing in common; you come from the ghetto. You couldn't get a better man to direct your picture."

"We're results of the ghetto," I said.

Josephson crushed the butt of his cigarette, tossed it into the ash tray. "What do you think of him?"

"Success is his meat, his drink, his reason for living. . . ."

"What's wrong with success? Don't all of us want it?"

"Success to Bern is making a lot of money," I said.

"Bern may not have your scruples, but he has the will to survive. He can put things over that you and I never can. Wait till you see him in action. . . ."

Josephson's deep insight, which had enabled him to work with Bern, revealed itself as he outlined his screen version of *Hungry Hearts*. He was able to see the humor behind the poverty that seemed to me so tragic.

For one of the scenes he suggested Gedalyeh Mindel, the erstwhile water-carrier from Plinsk putting on his Hester Street finery to meet his countrymen at Ellis Island. Patent-leather shoes with spats, a gold watch and chain across his stomach, the white shirt with a starched collar tight enough to choke him. A pushcart peddler of bananas putting on the airs of a new millionaire in America.

"I never thought that Gedalyeh Mindel was so funny," I laughed.

"Bern is as funny as your water carrier from Plinsk," Josephson said. "But instead of putting on Gedalyeh Mindel's starched shirt and gold watch and chain, he flaunts his million-dollar budget that'll 'knock their eyes out.' "

"You understand my ghetto so much better than I. People that I thought horrible have humor for you. . . ."

"Nobody is horrible when you understand him," Josephson said.

As we got deeper into the plot, Josephson visualized the boat steaming into the harbor, the load of immigrants crowding the steerage deck, listening in awed silence to one of the passengers while he read the words engraved on the Statue of Liberty:

> Give me your tired, your poor,
> Your huddled masses yearning to
>   breathe free,
> The wretched refuse of your teeming
>   shore.
> Send these, the homeless, tempest-
>   tossed, to me,
> I lift my lamp beside the golden door.

"Those lines are beautiful," I said, "but none of these

immigrants can read English, and they'd be too excited to listen. As the boat nears America they'd sing and dance, and laugh and weep for joy. They're living poetry!"

Josephson leaned an elbow on the arm of the chair, his hand covering his mouth, intent on what I was saying.

"You see," I went on, "the real thing creates its own poetry."

"Sometimes I have to write the wrong thing to see it is wrong," Josephson said.

In the stimulating collaboration with Josephson, my aversion to Paul Bern, my fear of my secretary, fled.

"Why do authors complain that Hollywood distorts their books, slaps on ready-made puppets to take the place of real characters?" I asked as Josephson gathered up his papers. "Your scenario has built up my character sketches into a story that every one can understand."

Color rushed into Josephson's pale face. "Say I'm a genius." He laughed. "My wife thinks I'm the world's worst fool when it comes to selling my talents. She complains that I'm the most underpaid underdog on the lot. I get so interested in my job, I haven't time or energy to work for a raise."

"I never dreamed that Hollywood had real people like you."

"Wait till you come to a rehearsal, see what Bern does with the actors—and you'll meet people who understand and respect their work."

When the scenario revisions were completed, Josephson showed me the different sets that were being assembled for *Hungry Hearts.* We walked out of the office building to the studio lots and saw an East Side tenement, the rusty fire escapes cluttered with bedding and washlines, a row of pushcarts that seemed to come directly from the Hester Street fish market, a whole city humming— a beehive of motion-picture industry.

Going through a narrow door, we came into a huge hall with stacks of scenery, a tangle of wires, and the smell of paint. Men in overalls were working on the thatched roofs of the little houses for the miniature village in Poland.

I was suddenly back in Plinsk. The past which I had struggled to suggest in my groping words was recreated here in straw and plaster. I stepped into one of these huts, touched the old battered cookstove, the benches scratched from wear, the feather beds piled high, covered with an old gray shawl. I closed my eyes and could almost see Mother spreading the red-checked Sabbath tablecloth. The steaming platter of *gefüllte* fish, the smell of fresh-baked *hallah*, Sabbath white bread. Mother blessing the lighted candles, ushering in the Sabbath.

"This interior is perfect," I said to Josephson. "But if there were only some way to suggest the constant shadow of fear that hung over our heads between these four walls. And the even greater fear of the Czar's pogroms that drove us back inside, the moment we stepped out."

"That will be up to the actors," Josephson said. "And Paul Bern will draw it out of them if any one can."

"But you are the architect of this play," I said. "You showed the funny side of Gedalyeh Mindel when he dressed up to meet his countrymen at Ellis Island. You've got to devise stage business that'll bring out the fear that these people breathe in with every breath they draw."

"Well, you're the author. You've got to produce the substance for the architect to work with."

"I've got it!" I cried, and I started to tell him a scene from my childhood. . . .

It was the day before Purim holiday in Plinsk. Mother was preparing the dinner, putting the potatoes on the stove to boil when the mothers of the children whom Father taught Hebrew came bearing Purim gifts. One proudly carried a platter of *gefüllte* fish, another a bottle of homemade raisin wine, others came with all kinds of buns.

Our living in Poland was precarious, even in the best

of times. In a village as poor as ours, who had money to pay the rabbi? Our bread was mostly donations—goodwill offerings—from poor people.

This shower of abundance inspired Mother with the holiday spirit. Though Purim was still a day off, she brought out her clean Sabbath apron. That clean apron always went to Mother's head like wine. The sparkle in her eyes lighted the room. "I might as well put on my whole holiday in honor of our good neighbors." She laughed, hiding her rags under her wedding shawl. (The shawl I had pawned for a quarter.) In her magnanimous mood Mother cut up one Purim cake into twenty pieces so that the children and neighbors could sample it. Twenty mouths had a sip out of one glass of wine.

Our voices rose joyously in the excitement of the coming feast. Mother, who could outcurse the Devil when worried for bread, and who could outwail all the mourners at a funeral, could also outshine all the young girls dancing the *kazatzka* at a wedding when she was happy.

She began to sing and dance the ancient Purim chant, carefree as a young girl: *"Vos mir sannen sannen mir, ober Iden sannen mir."* ("What we are that we are, but Jews, Jews we are.") We went on clapping our hands and stamping our feet to the rhythm of the dance. We were too full of holiday excitement to hear anything. All at once there was a banging at the door.

A club broke through the window, scattering glass over the table. Another club smashed the rest of the window. Mother rushed to bar the door. The children clung to her in terror.

"Oi weh!" Mother wrung her hands. "The Cossacks! And Father at the synagogue!"

We stood at the barred door in a panic, fearful for Father. To step outside would be suicide, but to remain inside, not knowing what was happening to him, was unendurable.

After an eternity of waiting, we heard Father's voice calling to us. The door was unbarred to let him in.

"Thank God! You're safe!" Mother cried, clinging to him.

"It was a pair of drunken *muzhiks*," Father said. "At the synagogue we were terror-stricken when they began pounding at the door, throwing stones through the windows. But we went on praying. Then, ready for the worst, we walked out together. They were sprawled in drunken sleep on the steps."

Mother turned to the table, looked at the broken glass on the *gefüllte* fish. "Our Purim feast is ruined." She burst out weeping.

"Woman!" Father admonished. "Instead of praising God we are still alive, you weep over *gefüllte* fish. We're in the land of bondage. . . ."

"We don't have to remain in bondage," I cried. "We can go to America."

Father and Mother looked at me and I went on like one possessed. "For what are we waiting? Another ukase from the Czar? Another pogrom?"

"America wills itself in her." Mother shook her head, but into her eyes had come the shine of dreams.

"Gedalyeh Mindel, that dummox, had sense enough to go to America," I went on. "Why can't we?" I turned to Father. "If Gedalyeh Mindel could become a businessman in America, what couldn't you do with all your Torah learning?"

"Listen to our crazy redhead." Father smiled indulgently. "When she begins to burn for a thing . . ."

Mother laughed into Father's eyes. "From where did she get her craziness and her red hair if not from you?"

The children formed a ring around Father and Mother, shouting, "Let's go to America!" And I shouted louder: "White bread and meat we'll eat every day in America! America!"

After Josephson had made some notes of the scene, we walked out of the mud hut, out of the village of Plinsk with all its fears.

"Now let's see the life in America," Josephson said, leading the way to another set, the interior of a tenement flat. He turned on the spluttering gas jet hanging from the middle of the low ceiling, showing the airless darkness. The broken plaster crumbling from the walls, the wooden washtub on a stool in the middle of the kitchen. The clotheslines with the patched underwear strung over the stove. I lifted the worn strip of oilcloth in front of the rusty iron sink, almost expecting to see cockroaches crawl out of their nests.

Then we came to the sweatshop with the grilled windows, the piles of shirts on the wooden tables. I sat down at one of the machines. It actually sewed. I looked up at Josephson.

"Would you believe it, I was the fastest operator in the shop? The foreman used me to set the pace."

"Is writing less of a grind than the sewing machine?"

"I was better and quicker at the sewing machine."

We walked to the next stage where a rehearsal was in progress. Bern was seated in a deep leather chair, his attention fixed on the young actress playing the part of Sara, the heroine of *Hungry Hearts*.

Sara, on her hands and knees, was scrubbing the rotting splintered floorboards of her flat in Hester Street. A knock at the door. A young man walked in. She stopped scrubbing, stood up, wiped her hands on her apron.

"I've come for the rent." He twisted his hat in his hands. "My uncle, the landlord . . ."

She looked at him, unable to believe that any one with so gentle a face could have anything to do with the hated landlord.

"You? Related to the *landlord?*"

His face turned red with embarrassment.

"He's my uncle, I work for him, so I can go to college. . . ."

"You go to *college?*"

He seemed to know the way she felt. His face brightened. "You'd like to study, too?"

"I might as well like the moon. I wanted to go to night school, but when I come home from the shop it's too late. The only time I got—Sundays——"

"I could help you on Sundays!" he said eagerly.

"You mean it?"

"Of course I mean it," he laughed. In a moment everything was simple. "May I come next Sunday?"

Uncle, landlord, rent forgotten, they looked at each other without speaking. Then, with a wave of his hat, he stumbled out.

She stared at the door through which he had gone. "Beautiful," she said over and over again.

Her mother, old and workworn, came in carrying a market basket. She took out a newspaper bundle of herring and a bag of potatoes and laid them on the table.

"Potatoes went up another cent on a pound! And meat is now only for millionaires! Eating is dearer than diamonds these days." Suddenly she looked at Sara. "Why are you crying?"

Sara only wept the harder.

"*Meshugeneh!* What's the matter with you?"

"Something wonderful happened!" Sara hugged herself, laughing through her tears. "Some one's going to teach me! Teach me English! I'll learn to be an American!"

Hungry Hearts had come to life before my eyes. I rushed forward and put my arms around Helen Ferguson, the young actress. "You made me relive what you were acting." I motioned to the others. "You're artists. . . ."

Bern looked at them with affectionate possessiveness. "I made them. I made them more real than life."

"Sure. He thinks he's God." Helen Ferguson laughed.

"You remind me of Kipling's lines," I said.

". . . No one shall work for money, and
no one shall work for fame;
But each for the joy of the working . . ."

"What's wrong with working for money and fame?"

Bern demanded. "What joy is there in working without money and without fame? I want money. I want fame. And I want plenty of it."

He flung his arms around the two actresses playing mother and daughter. "You think these two are working for love? They want money, and they want it as much as I do." Bern laughed. "We look like one happy family, don't we? Do you know how these bastards are fighting for every inch of film? Wait till the rushes come in. This loving mother and daughter will be clawing each other's throats for camera angles. Christ! Do you know what it takes to get this bunch of egomaniacs to work together?"

It was long past dinnertime but, regardless of time, Bern went on with the rehearsal.

"Why don't you give them a chance to eat?" I said to Bern. "They're tired."

"I don't care if they drop dead all around me. We got to get it right."

"But they're hungry. I know I'm hungry. . . ."

"To hell with them! They're paid to work. And they got to come across even if we stay here all night."

My old sweatshop boss had nothing on Bern. But it was an unforgettable experience to watch him at work. Whipping the actors with curses and invectives one minute, the next hugging and cajoling them, but getting out of each and every one of them the last ounce of response.

As I walked off the set with Josephson, a boy came up with a letter, an invitation from Rupert Hughes for dinner next evening.

I was elated. I showed the note to Josephson. "The first time in my life that a real author asked me to eat at his home."

"Why not? You're the poor girl who struck it rich. The personification of the happy ending that Hollywood has been turning out."

"What about the stars Hollywood turns out?" I asked.

"In our factory here we turn out stars of our own brand. But you're some one outside Hollywood, a character from the real world that makes our factory stories of success seem valid."

"Success is such a joke applied to me." I laughed.

I knew only too well it was not me that had been invited to this dinner, but the "Sweatshop Cinderella" the papers had made of me. But I was as excited as a young girl going to her first party.

═══════════════════════════════════════

CHAPTER IV

IMPORTANT PEOPLE

LEANING AGAINST the cushions of the car that was taking me to the home of Rupert Hughes, I caught sight of my straggling hair in the mirror. I smoothed it back as best I could. I looked down at my plain blue serge skirt, my thick-soled sandals. Why had I never dressed like other women? It wasn't just a matter of being poor. The poorest shopgirl with her mind on style managed to look as smart as other shopgirls. I never could or would fit into the up-to-date clothes that everybody else wore. Even now when I no longer had to search through bargain basements, now that I had money enough to shop at the best stores, perversity made me cling to my push-cart clothes. Even in Hollywood I wanted to be myself —whatever that was.

But you're no longer scrubbing floors or punching a machine, I told myself. You're on your way to meet who's who in Hollywood, about to be initiated into the sacred circle of "eminent authors." I looked at my hands, bitten with the sharp red and gray of work. Why didn't you celebrate the great event, treat yourself to a manicure? Do you have to look like a *yenteh* from Hester Street to be yourself?

Immediately the other side of me protested. What's wrong with looking like Hester Street? I am Hester Street. Why should I be afraid to be what I am? Why should I dress up to meet them? Would they dress down to meet me? The familiar feel of the creases in my blouse, my unpolished shoes, the shine of my old skirt reassured me that with all the change around me, I was still unchanged. I was still myself.

But can you be yourself with the money from the movies tucked safely in the bank? You're afraid to spend your money and you're afraid to give it up. You're afraid to plunge back into the poverty and dirt from which money has saved you. Yet you fear what money may do to you. You want to be a person of importance. You want to be a success—and yet you can't give up what you were when you were nobody. You want too much.

The sun was beginning to set, weaving circles of light over the tall Hawaiian pines of Beverly Hills. Never had I seen skies so blue, grass so green. The toy houses and fairylike gardens that I glimpsed as the car sped along added a fantastic setting to my dreams of the fellowship of writers.

The chauffeur turned the car up a graveled drive lined with exotic trees and shrubs. He stopped before a villa as plain as a New England farmhouse.

I walked up to the porch, and then paused in sudden doubt of myself. All my instincts cried: Don't! Don't go in! Run! Make your escape before any one sees you. You don't belong here.

But this was my first chance to see the other world. Even if it killed me, I had to see, I had to know what it was like. I hid behind a rosebush and looked in. Men in tails and women in low-necked evening gowns stood around talking.

I recognized Will Rogers, Elinor Glyn, Gertrude Atherton, Katharine Newlin Burt, Alice Duer Miller. I had seen their pictures in the Sunday papers, authors of the latest best sellers, their names printed in big letters on the covers of popular magazines.

The makers of best sellers! Fear and awe of success fought within me. To my frightened eyes the authors in that drawing room looked like conquering gods towering over me. Who was I to have ventured among them? One book, and only a pitiful tale of myself at that— A writer? Never had I felt so hopelessly out of place.

"You don't own the dirt under their doorsteps." Words with which my mother had crushed the courage out of me as a child rushed over me, barring that door.

They had invited me. They had made the overtures. I tried to reason, but it was no use. I could not bridge the gap between myself and the celebrities in that drawing room.

I turned to flee just as Rupert Hughes opened the door.

"We've been waiting for you. And here you are, standing us up——"

"I was scared to come in!"

He put his arm around me and laughed as a grownup laughs at a child. His easy, affable smile melted the arrogance with which I had armed myself when I started out in my old clothes. They told me he was the richest, the most versatile of the Hollywood authors. He was a musician, a journalist, a historian, and movie producer. And yet, none of the airs of the big shot about him. He was a short, solidly built man, his head close to his heart.

"I'd like you to meet my wife," he said, introducing a slender, dark-haired woman.

"So glad to have you with us." She smiled, her glance sweeping over me in swift appraisal.

As in a dream, I was aware of some one taking my hand and guiding me to the foyer where a maid helped me take off my hat and coat. And then I stepped on a carpet of air, into a room of dim, golden light. Faces gleamed to me out of the shadows, luminous, ephemeral. Where had I seen this visionary place before? I had seen it when I was in the dark hold of the steerage, on the way to America, when I was sewing buttons in a factory, when I walked the streets trying to feed my hunger with dreams of my rise in the world.

"How do you like Hollywood?" some one asked.

"It's so different," I said, shocked by the shrillness of

my voice. "There was a freezing blizzard when I left New York. And when I got here, I walked into sunshine and flowers. It's all so unreal. . . ."

"We New Yorkers think no place is real but New York," Alice Duer Miller said with her warm smile.

"We New Yorkers!" She was including me in her circle, treating me as if I belonged to it! If I could only tell her what it meant to be among fellow writers who understood all I was trying to be!

Release from fear and anxiety spread a healing glow of good will in me toward all these lovely, important people. My lifelong hatred for the rich, the successful, turned to servile gratitude for their friendliness. In my eagerness to become like them, with the ardor of a convert to a new faith, I repudiated all that I had been. The poor, I thought, were too submerged in the fight for bread to indulge in the amenities of life. Success made people kinder, nobler, more beautiful. Only the rich had the leisure, the peace of mind to take an interest in one another.

I could almost feel my father turn in his grave in horror at my apostasy. His own daughter losing her soul for a rich woman's smile! I could almost see him step into the drawing room and shake a warning finger at me. "Can fire and water be together? Neither can godliness and ease."

Your godliness is for the dying, the renegade in me retorted. I'm young. I'm going to have all that the poor never had. I'll be at ease in Zion. I'll have riches, fame, success—all the fullness of the earth—and heaven too.

I took up a glass of sherry and swallowed all of it. The pleasant warmth of the drink gave me the courage to look around. My hand ran over the arm of my chair to feel the texture of the fabric. The rug on the floor, the paintings on the wall, the mellow lights of the lamps—colors and lines of everything flowed into one another. Flowers on old mahogany, long-stemmed glasses on silver trays, perfumes blending with cigarette smoke. But what bewitched me most was the gaiety of these people, the ease with which they enjoyed the moment, as if it would last forever.

I turned to Mrs. Miller standing beside me. "I read your last story in the *Post*," I said. "You have such velvet smoothness of style. When you write, it's as if you sat back in an easy chair in the front parlor of your mind, where everything is in perfect order."

She smiled away my enthusiasm. "I've been a mathematics teacher. Mathematics has given me a sense of proportion. When I write, the plot comes out complete like a baby out of its mother's womb."

"Oh! How I envy your clarity!" I said. "And the ease with which you turn out one novel after another. I never know what I'm trying to write until it's written. Then begins the labor of cutting to clarify the meaning. I never know whether what I cut out isn't better than what I left in——"

"Every writer has to find his own way of working. I think out every word of my novels before I begin. Then I type them with practically no revisions."

No revisions! I stared at her, trying to imagine what life would be like without wrestling with each living word.

"The trouble with me," said Elinor Glyn, "my plots come spinning so fast I don't take time to develop the characters."

I turned from her to Rupert Hughes. "Can you shake your stories out of your sleeve too?"

"My plots don't spin at all." He laughed. "How about you, Miss Yezierska?"

"I can never learn to plot or plan. It's always a mystery to me how I ever work out a beginning or an end of a story."

My glass refilled, I gulped it down, forgetting I was not drinking water, and went on talking. People from other parts of the room came over. The little common sense left in the back of my head cried: Stop! Don't make a fool of yourself. Don't walk out naked for these people.

But the words kept coming. "I only want to take the hurt out of my heart when I write. But the minute my pencil touches paper, I begin to worry how to write instead of going ahead and writing. And I become stiff and self-conscious. Is it the fear of being a foreigner that makes me want to explain myself so much? But I've had moments when I was so filled with the life I've lived I felt myself flow out into my words. These rare moments when I was my real self, I took back the fraud, the humbug, like God absolving the Prodigal."

Rupert Hughes took my arm and led the way into the dining room. We seated ourselves around a table gleaming with silver and fine linen. For once in my life I was where I wanted to be. For once I was part of everything. It was all I could do not to let my head sink on the table and weep. I wanted to weep and I wanted to clap my hands and sing and shout. "I've arrived! I'm in with Hollywood royalty! Behold! Pushcart clothes and all— I am the guest of honor at the feast!"

The table reeling, dancing a jig, champagne floating in foam, roast squabs with lace-paper frills on their legs —and me in my old clothes, the star of the evening—that's America.

"What are you thinking of?" Mr. Hughes asked.

"Ask me when I'm sober."

"Why be sober?" And he motioned the waiter to refill my glass with champagne.

"How's your picture going?" Mrs. Hughes asked.

"It's going to be the greatest picture of the century." I heard myself repeat Paul Bern's boast. "The *Uncle Tom's Cabin* of the immigrant."

"Have another drink," some one said. "If you have enough champagne you'll believe anything they tell you."

I noticed Alice Duer Miller smiling across the table. Was she laughing at me? Her smile made me suddenly feel the gulf between us. And now, beginning to doubt again, my ears caught snatches of conversation that widened and deepened that gulf.

"When I sell the movie rights, I get all the money I can out of them, and never bother to see the picture. . . ."

"Only the title of my last book was used. I can sell it again—change names of the characters—change the setting. . . ."

"Royalties? Poison ivy. Don't touch it. Get all you can get. But get it in cash. Sign anything they give you. What's the difference? Contracts don't mean a thing. . . ."

"I wasn't the first to cash in on the gold rush in Alaska. But I had the goods when the market was soaring. I knew Alaska and had facts to boost my fiction."

I pushed the empty wine glass from me. I had dreamed of Olympian gods and woke up among hucksters. I remembered seeing Shakespeare's *Merchant of Venice* in modern dress. Now I saw the fish market in evening clothes. The fight that went on at the pushcarts in Hester Street went on in this Hollywood drawing room.

Loneliness oppressed me. Even if I turned myself inside out, I could not compete with the sharp, shrewd barter of those business authors. If I could not stand haggling and bargaining for pennies at the pushcarts, how could I stand this movie market where the bargaining for contracts and royalties was multiplied into fabulous thousands of dollars?

When some of the guests were beginning to leave, I went for my hat and coat. Will Rogers stopped me. "See here, gal! Can I give you a lift home?"

I looked at his farmer's sunburned face with the funny flop of hair hanging over his forehead, his laughing eyes.

"How does all this fuss and feathers hit you, sister?" he asked, putting his hand on my shoulder.

"Is this Hollywood's Four Hundred?" I asked. Then, noticing his blue flannel shirt, I shook a finger at him. "You, too, dared to crash into society without evening clothes?"

His laughter was as refreshing as sunlight and mountain air. I laughed with him as I never had before.

"Come on, gal! I can't say your name." He took my arm and led me to his car.

CHAPTER V

THE MYTH THAT MADE HOLLYWOOD

AFTER MY début into Hollywood society Will Rogers invited me to visit his family at his Santa Monica ranch. Like millions of people throughout the country, I used to read Rogers' column in *The New York Times* and his adventures as "The Self-Appointed Ambassador of Good-Will" in *The Saturday Evening Post*. But I did not know his power until I had heard him speak to the Jewish Actors' Guild on behalf of Eddie Cantor's camp for poor boys' free vacations. He said that there were certain things that no money could buy, that only the privileged poor could enjoy. When he had visited Eddie's camp he had been so impressed he wanted his own boy to spend a summer there. But no money could buy admission to Eddie's happy hunting grounds for kids. Talk about the privileges of poverty! Any poor kid had a chance to enjoy the luxuries denied to the rich!

An Oklahoma cowboy, with his simple gift of fellowship, he had that hallful of people in the palm of his hand. With his power to impart his ease, his joy in life, he made a crowd of Jews laugh away their heritage of sorrow.

The same spirit that had impelled Rogers to speak in behalf of the poor boys' camp made him go out of his way to befriend me. He saw how lost I was in Hollywood and had invited me to spend a week end with his wife and children. I felt I must celebrate the occasion in some special way. All at once my old clothes could no longer contain me. I was letting myself go into a new world. New clothes were part of this new world! I was going to enjoy all the things I had done without, but enjoy people most of all. I decided to go shopping with my secretary. She would know her way about when it came to clothes.

She was waiting for me as usual in the inner room of my office. I was in such a magnanimous mood I could not only forgive Miss Young her youth, her beauty, but even find pleasure in her company. I was getting used to my secretary as I was getting used to my private car and chauffeur.

"It's a grand day," I said.

Her head was bent over her typewriter. She seemed not to see or hear me.

"What perfect weather!" I took off my gloves. "Doesn't it ever rain here?"

She gave me a quick glance and began dusting the typewriter. I looked at her slim young legs in sheer silk stockings and patent-leather pumps. She wore a blouse and skirt with the grace and style of a French model.

"I'm going shopping today," I said. "Come along. Show me where you buy your clothes. You have such good taste."

"A lot of good it does me."

"What's the matter?" I asked.

For the first time she looked at me.

"Try getting a five-dollar raise and being told a hundred girls are waiting to step into your shoes," she said. "All I get is twenty-five dollars a week—and on that I have to look like a fashion plate!"

"You mean to say you're making only twenty-five a week? How can you dress the way you do?"

"I'm part of the stage-set," she said bitterly. "If I didn't dress the part, I'd lose my job——"

The bones in her face stood out sharply under her make-up. Perhaps she had not had enough to eat that morning, but she had covered hunger with the paint of a beauty parlor. When I had been poor I had walked about in rags. But this girl had to wear silk stockings, have her hair waved, nails manicured—on twenty-five dollars a week. This dressed-up poverty was as different from the poverty I had known as Hollywood was different from the ghetto.

"You need more than a diploma from a business college to hold down this job——"

"I'll speak to the personnel manager about you at once," I told her and phoned for an appointment.

Without stopping to think what I would say, I went to his office. He rose from his huge desk, turned on his executive smile.

"What can I do for you?" He drew up a chair for me.

"My secretary . . ." I began, wilted by the slick business face.

"Isn't she okay?"

"More than okay. Why don't you give her a raise?"

He relit his cigar, took a few puffs, his eyes following the smoke to the ceiling. "My job is to run the office force with economy and efficiency. Wages are a matter of supply and demand. So many girls flock to Hollywood, they're begging to work for less than twenty a week. . . ."

"But how can they exist on those wages? Their clothes cost so much."

"Don't let it get you." He smiled. "She's only a stenographer. There are millions of them. If they want to dress like the stars, it's their hard luck."

The smile on his self-satisfied face sickened me. He ate up the air, ate the words out of my mouth.

"The picture business is a game," he said importantly. "The toughest game in the world. Those who can't take it had better get out."

Smoking his cigar, he reminded me of my first boss in the shirt factory. I had protested against overtime work without pay. "Nightwork for nothing is too much."

I was immediately fired for my moment's rebellion.

And now in Hollywood it seemed I had merely reversed

my position, joined hands with those who grew rich at the expense of the poor.

I walked cut, feeling like a dumb, bewildered immigrant again. And then I remembered the friendly talk I had had with Will Rogers the night before. He would know how to help my secretary get her raise.

I had an appointment with Elinor Glyn for lunch that day in the studio dining room where Rogers often ate. Hurrying to meet her, I passed the "Bear Pit," the cafeteria where the anonymous small fry struggled with their trays at the steam tables. Beyond this noisy crowd was the dining room where the box-office names, the stars, directors, authors, were served by obsequious waiters who catered to their individual diets.

Miss Glyn was waiting for me at her table.

"It's nice to see you again," she said, holding out her hand.

Will Rogers sauntered over. His presence seemed to fling open all the windows of the room.

"We got the barn ready for your visit next Friday," he said.

"Only the barn? I thought, since you're the mayor of Santa Monica, I'd stay in City Hall. I was going to get a new outfit for the occasion. But if I'm to stay at the barn, my old clothes are good enough."

"Well, if you're coming in your glad rags we'll have to put you in the parlor." He threw a piece of chewing gum in his mouth. "Mind if I eat with you?" he asked.

"Come, sit down," I said. "I'm in great need of your advice."

"Where's the fire now, gal?"

I told him of the time I had wasted trying to persuade the personnel manager to raise Miss Young's salary.

"Relax," said Will Rogers. "How about some chow?"

"I'd rather talk than eat——"

"Go ahead and talk, but me—I'm eating." Rogers laughed, reaching for a roll.

Still smarting from my encounter with the personnel

manager, I went on: "Did you ever meet a man you hated at sight?"

"I never met a man I didn't like," he said.

"You never met a man you didn't like?" I looked at him. He was so pleasing to people because he found them so pleasant. His sunburned face had the vitality of a man unacquainted with grief, unaware of defeat. He had been unanimously elected mayor of his town. He loved his wife. He worshiped his children. He was such a perfect salesman of himself he could have become a self-satisfied citizen, but he had never stopped being himself—a warm human being.

"When I was a kid on the farm the cow hands usta talk about mean horses or stubborn yearlings. But I never met a calf or any other critter I didn't understand and that didn't understand me. I saw mighty little difference between 'em. Some was more ornery, and some less, but I got along with 'em all."

"Could you get along with them all in a crowded tenement in Hester Street?"

"We-l-l-l," he spun out slowly, "I never lived in Hester Street, but folks are pretty much the same in Hester Street or Kalamazoo. . . ."

Elinor Glyn turned to me, laughing. "He loves everybody, the way the clown loves his audience, the human material for his wisecracks."

"All of us here are clowning for pay, except people like my secretary," I said.

"And what are you clowning for?" the gum-chewing philosopher demanded. "For the glory of the woiking goil?"

Miss Glyn straightened the silver at her plate with carefully manicured fingers. The royal lift of her head declared she lived in an orderly world where values were fixed.

"Something is wrong when my secretary, with her youth and intelligence, has it so hard—" I went on.

"After all, you got here," said Elinor Glyn.

"I got here by an odd streak of luck," I said.

"Don't be a sourpuss," Rogers admonished. "Don't mock our faith in good luck, or you'll destroy the myth that made Hollywood."

"You could give your secretary a raise out of your own pocket, if it would make you feel better," Elinor Glyn said. "But would that solve the problem of the others?"

Rogers shook his finger and winked at me. "You ought to know that poverty develops character. Don't weaken the girl's fiber with charity. Blessed are the poor. For them is the kingdom."

Everything he said weakened the kinship that the wine and the cocktails had made me feel the night before.

I looked at Elinor Glyn's queenlike neck and shoulders. Here was a woman against whom fate had no weapons. As for Rogers, he laughed so easily. But why shouldn't he laugh? He had no need to change himself, no urge to change the world.

I watched the relish with which he swallowed his last morsel of deep-dish apple pie. Elinor Glyn daintily spooned whipped cream and cherry from her parfait glass. They ate with pleasure. They lived with pleasure.

For a moment I felt I was watching a scene from my past when I had stood outside Childs Restaurant window, seeing the flapjacks turn golden-brown on the griddle—for others to eat.

"Sad, sad, sad little sister." Rogers patted my cheek. "You got success on a tear-jerker the hard way. Must you fiddle the same tune forever? Suppose you give us another number?"

"Have you ever wanted what you couldn't be, or what you couldn't do?"

Rogers took a gulp of water and flung his napkin on the table.

"Gal! You're like a punch-drunk prize fighter, striking an opponent no longer there. You've won your fight and you don't know it. . . ."

"How long has it been since you were poor?" I asked.

"Not so long ago," Rogers retorted. "But I gave them what they wanted. You did too. Lap up the cream while the going's good."

That afternoon when I walked out on the lot, the chauffeur was waiting for me as usual. He opened the door of the car. I was about to step in, but the fine upholstery, the neatly folded rug, and the chauffeur in his smooth-fitting uniform made me feel as if I were part of a stage-set.

"How can I get back to my hotel by trolley?" I asked.

"The trolley is a long roundabout way," he said. "I can get you back in forty minutes——"

"I don't want the car. Give me directions for the trolley."

Outside the gates of the studio. I joined the crowd waiting for the trolley: stagehands, stenographers, nameless office workers who punched the clock morning and night. It was like the warmth of an open log fire after the artificial fireplace in my office. Here's where I belong, I thought. I felt myself relax, for the first time at ease in Hollywood. When the trolley finally arrived, every seat was jammed. I squeezed in among the straphangers, stimulated by the crowdedness, the physical discomfort. On one side of me, a big-boned Negro washwoman; on the other, a grimy mechanic, a lifetime's hard labor in the lines of his face.

Before the trip was half over, I was exhausted. If I could only slump into a seat. And then a man in front of me got up. Before I had a chance to sit down, a Mexican day laborer pushed past me into the seat. A smell of garlic and the sickening odor of sweat turned my stomach. Too weary to hold onto the strap any longer, I surrendered to the pitching and tossing of the crowd at every turn of the trolley. At last, after many stops, we got to West Los Angeles station, just as the bus to Santa Monica began to pull out. I had missed my connection by less than a minute. The next bus would not be due for half an hour. Another half-hour of waiting in this noisy, pushing mob was too much. Confused, unnerved by the roaring traffic, I hailed a taxi.

As I watched the meter tick off the dimes and dollars, I began to laugh at my silly, stupid contradictions. What a fool and a faker I was to think that giving up the car and riding in the trolley would still my guilty conscience!

CHAPTER VI

NOT A WOMAN—NOT A WRITER

THE MORNING they began shooting *Hungry Hearts,*
Sam Goldwyn came on the set and took a seat next to
me. While the klieg lights were being arranged he asked,
"What's the next thing you'll write?"

"It's going to be called *Children of Loneliness,*" I said.
"This is the first time a title came to me before the story
was written."

I told him how, long ago, the words had waked me out
of sleep. I had taken the pencil and paper I kept under
my pillow and written them quickly in the faint light that
seeped through the curtainless window from the moon-
lit sky. Then, just as I had started to fall asleep again,
the middle of a scene had come to me with such force
that I had to go on writing. A million invisible knots with
which I had been bound loosed themselves in writing the
words. When I finally fell asleep, I had slept so soundly
the alarm clock could not wake me. These formless, in-
coherent flashes of feeling about the story still pursued
me even in Hollywood.

"Hollywood sunshine will do the trick," Goldwyn
laughed. "It'll pop out like mushrooms overnight. . . ."

"I have been too much on the go since I came to Hollywood to think it out," I said. "Thought grows in silence."

"Well, then, come to the lunchroom where we can chat,"
he said, with a compelling smile.

I was flattered at the casual way he took my arm and
asked me to lunch. When I looked at him across the

table, he was so friendly I forgot that he was such a big shot that every one in the room watched us.

"How about a cocktail—and *borscht* for our first course?" Goldwyn asked.

Before I could answer, he gave the order to the waiter, then turned back to me. "What's your new story about?"

"I've written only fragments of scenes. I can't talk about it till I get to the end——"

"I don't know much about literature," Goldwyn said, lighting a cigarette. "But I do know that a plot of a good story can be summed up in a sentence, and you must know the end of the plot before you begin——"

"I never know the end of a story when I begin." I enjoyed talking back to him. "My characters spin their own plots. And the end of a plot is as much of a mystery to me as a detective thriller."

"But there's no mystery in what you've already written. Out with it!"

"On the surface it's a double-murder story."

Goldwyn looked at me in amused surprise. "Are you switching from immigrants to crime thrillers?"

"Oh, no," I laughed. "Not that kind of a murder story —a Hester Street murder——"

"But what's the plot? The suspense?"

"Suspense? What greater suspense is there than the mystery of a guilty conscience?"

He flicked the ash off his cigarette. "Well, get to the point. What's the plot?"

"The plot is the expiation of guilt."

Under Goldwyn's silent gaze I paused uncomfortably, groping for the explanation. "I had to break away from my mother's cursing and my father's preaching to live my life; but without them I had no life. When you deny your parents, you deny the ground under your feet, the sky over your head. You become an outlaw, a pariah."

I pushed away the coffee. It spilled on the tablecloth. Throwing my napkin over the brown stain, I went on: "They mourned me as if I were dead. I am like Cain, forever bound to the brother he slew with his hate."

Goldwyn squashed his cigarette. He looked at me from far away, hiding behind his unsmiling business eyes, and yet I could not stop talking. The words that I could not write now rushed from me without control.

"And now, here I am—lost in chaos, wandering between worlds——"

I saw in Goldwyn's face how mad I sounded. He simply had asked me for the plot of my next story and I had turned it into an intimate confession.

"When you get it set in your mind, let me know," he said, standing up. "Come and see me next Monday." And he fled.

I watched his retreating figure, feeling empty, deflated, slapped in the face with my own folly. It was as though I had punched a hole in myself and let part of me spill into the sand.

You've made a fool of yourself again! I wept inwardly, sick with self-disgust. I felt like the woman who went to a doctor for a diagnosis. He treated her pregnancy for tumor, and the child was born an idiot. Here I was for the first time an author among authors, a newcomer among Hollywood's great, treated by the expert Goldwyn to a private story conference. But my obsession with my murderous ego, which had driven people from me in Hester Street, now was catching up with me in Hollywood.

When I got back to my office, Miss Young looked up and said, "I heard you had lunch with Goldwyn."

A feeling of guilt swept over me for having forgotten all about her.

"I'll give you the five-dollar raise," I said quickly.

"Oh, thank you! That's wonderful!" And she bent over the typewriter to hide her emotion.

I glanced at her as she typed my letters with her sure, competent touch. A good stenographer. A perfect typist. She was better equipped to look out for herself than I. She had a job. A definite trade. She had self-respect. She had security.

She tapped her life away, day after day, with the self-confidence of automatic efficiency. She had never been tempted to go beyond herself. A business education fitted her for life. She knew her niche in the world. I was like Mohammed's coffin, suspended between heaven and hell.

Miss Young stopped typing, glanced at the clock, then turned to me. "If you don't need anything more, may I go home? I have to meet some one."

I watched her clear her desk. Every paper orderly in its pigeonhole. With the same instinctive orderliness, she took her mirror and compact out of her purse, touched her nose with the powder puff, carefully reddened her lips and gave a final pat to her perfectly waved hair.

The door closed behind her. Her work was done. She was free to go out and enjoy herself. I was never done. For me there was no day and no night.

The telephone rang shrilly through the silent office. I picked up the receiver. It was a man's voice, asking for Miss Young. The same voice that was always calling her. No doubt he was waiting to take her home. Her job was only a temporary stopgap. Marriage was waiting for her. She would have all the things that should come naturally to a woman. The same efficiency with which she served as a secretary would serve her in all the human relationships that fulfill a woman's life. But I wanted the impossible of life, of love. And so I stood empty, homeless --outside of life. Not a woman—not a writer.

▰▰▰▰▰▰▰▰▰▰▰▰▰▰▰▰▰▰▰▰▰▰▰▰▰▰▰▰▰▰▰

CHAPTER VII

MY LIFE—A COLUMN A DAY

MY CONFERENCE with Goldwyn reminded me of a Hester Street story about a pious old Jewess terrified of what would happen to her after death. The last ritual, the Hebrew death prayer, was still on her lips: "Hear, O Israel! The Lord our God, the Lord is One . . ." when suddenly she produced a crucifix from under her pillow and kissed it.

The Jews threw up their hands at the sacrilege. *"Oi weh! Gevalt!* What a sin for God!"

"For God I have no fear," the old woman murmured. "God knows what's in the heart, but—just to be on the safe side——"

How often had I dug up from my hiding place of fear my secret crucifix—just to be on the safe side. In trying to win the approval of Hollywood, I was losing my own hard-won bit of truth.

The story I had betrayed to Goldwyn stuck in my throat. I couldn't swallow it, and I couldn't spit it out. I no longer believed in it. The importance had gone from it. And yet it stood between me and the life around me.

The effort to keep my secretary busy any longer was too much of a strain. I gave her the day off. Perhaps alone I might be able to work.

As she was leaving I noticed a book under her arm. "What are you reading?" I asked.

"Three Weeks by Elinor Glyn." She hugged the book.

"Oh, it's really a wonderful story. So exciting! I love it."

At the door she turned. "Thanks for letting me off. Now I can finish making my evening gown. I'm going to a dance Saturday night."

I thought of my own working days at Cohen's Shirt Factory. How greedily I would have clutched at a day off. Dresses, beaux, dances—the things other girls wanted, I also wanted. But over and above all, I wanted to learn. I could not put into words all I meant by wanting to learn. My dumbness was eating my heart out. I craved learning as a thing imprisoned in darkness craves light.

One evening, coming home from work, I saw through the basement window Minnie, the janitor's daughter, bent over her schoolbooks. Ach! I thought enviously, if I could only get hold of her books. What could I offer her? All week long Mother waited for my wages. Every penny went to pay back bills to the grocer. But this week I had earned fifty cents extra for sweeping the shop after the girls left.

With the courage of a capitalist, I walked up to the window. "Say, Minnie! What are you learning?"

"Synonyms," she grumbled.

"Synonyms? What's that?"

"It's words about words——"

"I'm crazy for words!" I bounced into the basement, seized the book from her hand. Words about words weren't just words to me. Each new word was a new ray of light in the dungeon of my dumbness. Synonyms spread before my eyes a feast of language. I put the book down on the table, tore open my pay envelope.

"Look!" I waved a shining half-dollar before her eyes. "All this is yours if you tell me everything you learn in school."

And so my education began. Evenings, Sundays, and holidays, I labored over Minnie's schoolbooks. A nickel a lesson, ten lessons for fifty cents bought me the right to read all her books. I became so elated with my progress that I raised the tuition fee to ten cents a lesson. Later on, when I earned more, I paid as high as a quarter for two lessons. When it came to learning, I loved to pay with a full hand.

As I learned English, I learned to piece together thoughts and feelings about the people around me. After the long day at the machine I could not rest, I could not sleep, till I unburdened on paper the ache of my confusion. I wrote half in Yiddish, half in English, feeling my way in the new language.

Everything that happened to me was a challenge that drove me to write. I turned to my writing the first thing in the morning and the last thing at night—as Father had turned to his prayers.

In my elation I read what I wrote to the girls in the shop during lunch. I watched their faces as I read. A stray word, a lift of an eyelid, a droop of the mouth told me where it was alive or dead.

When the girls in the shop were fed up with my story I found that Zalmon, the fish peddler, would listen, then Sopkin, the butcher. One day Hayim Shmerel, the plumber, came to fix the toilet. He had intelligent eyes. I read my story to him. He knew the language well enough to point out where my English was too Jewish.

Revisions that kept the parts I was working on ever new and exciting to me bored my listeners. Once they knew what the story was about they fled at my approach. But Sara Solomon, whose machine was next to mine, got the brunt of the torment that obsessed me.

"Only tell me a better word," I pleaded. "A better way of saying it——"

"I should write your stuff for you? If I knew how, I'd write my own." She turned to another girl with a jeering laugh. "A writer she wants to be yet!"

The ridicule plunged me back into the doubt and fear with which I had run to them for reassurance. And then I heard of a short-story course being given at the settlement house. I went to the teacher with all my hopes and fears in the typewritten bundle I held out to him.

He scanned it hastily. "This is emotional hodgepodge —not a story," he said. "A story must have a beginning, a middle, and an end."

"But this is my life. Where I began is no clearer to me than where I'll end. I thought by writing out what I don't know and can't understand, it would stop hurting me."

Irritation showed on his face. "A story must have a plot, otherwise it's no story——"

"What would be the good of writing unless I wrote what I felt, the way I felt it? Why must I squeeze myself into a plot?"

He shoved the pages across the desk. "So you think you're clever enough to discard the rules and create your own form?"

For weeks, months, I struggled by myself. Then, driven again by my need for approval, I returned to the teacher.

"Have you something new to show me?" he asked.

I held out a revised version of the old story. He read only the first page. "Start something new," he said. "Forget this."

"Can you forget about prison if you're in it? This story is my prison——"

"It's time you made a jail break," he laughed.

"You don't know what I'm talking about——"

"Then why do you come to me?"

I walked away, swallowing the shame of my beggary, whipped into obstinate persistence to go on writing. Nothing would stop me. I'd live my life writing and rewriting my story. The story of immigrants as helpless as deaf-mutes—children who came seeking the life of America and found themselves in the dead end of the sweatshop.

In defiance of the teacher's advice, I began sending the stories to the magazines. Before long, rejection slips became interspersed with an occasional letter of response.

"If you could only learn to overcome your bitterness," wrote one editor. "Life isn't as black as you paint it."

Then one day I saw my first story in print. Twenty-five

dollars. . . ! I gave up my job and set out on my writing career.

And here I was—in the mecca of writers—struck dumb. Like King Midas, whose touch turned everything to gold, I was dying of starvation.

I began walking about the room to rouse myself from the opiate of introspection. How thrilled I had been that first day when I saw my name printed on the door!

I opened my desk, pulled out the typewriter, the drawers stacked full of paper. All the paraphernalia for writing seemed as unreal as the artificial flame in the artificial fireplace. The delicate smell of orange blossoms, mingling with the perfume of roses, drifted in through the sunny windows. But the scent was synthetic. The sunshine weighted down with lead.

If there was at least one person to whom I could confide the terror of my impotence!

The door opened. Mr. Lenz stuck his head in. "I know I shouldn't interrupt, but I had to. Just for a moment."

"Come in." I gathered up my papers, glad to break the nightmare.

"A newspaper syndicate wants the story of your life," Lenz announced. "It took weeks. But, by God, I sold them the idea!"

He was jubilant with the hustling zeal of a happy missionary. I wondered why he should thrive on the same-sounding brass of ballyhoo that had silenced me.

"The story of my life is a big order," I hedged. "It would take me a lifetime to write it. . . ."

"Don't worry. We'll do the writing. All I want is facts."

I looked at him dumfounded.

"We have a swell news angle," he went on. "A college professor compiling a textbook of American literature is using your story to illustrate the opportunity America offers to every ambitious immigrant. We'll add Hollywood's touch to that. If you have anything to offer, Hollywood can use it. Hollywood, the golden city of opportunity, the first to recognize genius whether it comes from

Russia, Poland, or even the United States. Get it? If we build it around this opportunity angle, it'll have a terrific mass appeal. Editors will love it. See?"

"I see," I said. "But all my previous interviews were distortions. . . ."

"What do you care as long as you're in the spotlight? When they stop talking about you, that's the time to worry. I can turn out your life—a column a day."

He sat on my desk, picked up pad and pencil.

"Now for facts," he demanded.

"Facts?" I drew away.

"Oh, come on! How old are you?"

"I don't know."

"My God! You don't know your age? Another one of those . . ."

I was embarrassed. "I don't know my age," I cried out. "My mother had too many children, too many worries for bread, to keep track of when we were born."

He looked me over appraisingly. "I'd say you were about thirty-five."

"I'll say I am about thirty," I said.

"I'm sorry," he apologized. He looked at me again. "Your red hair and your skin are young, but your eyes are as old as trouble. Where were you born?"

"Plinsk. A part of Poland that belonged to Russia."

He stood up and faced me. "How did you ever get into this country?"

"A sweatshop boss in New York needed new hands for his machines. My mother had ten children. . . ."

"By golly! You've hit it!" He went on, with a new enthusiasm. "I've got my lead. I've got your dossier in our files. I can fill out the rest of your story. A natural for the tabloids! Millions couldn't buy this build-up for the picture."

This brain storm swept him out of the room.

He'd fill out the rest of my story. A column a day— the immigrant, with the bundle on her back, parading the legend of success in America!

As long as I remained with Goldwyn I was in a glass-house with crooked mirrors. Every move I made was distorted, and every distortion exploited to further the sale of *Hungry Hearts*. The dinner parties, the invitations to speak at churches, synagogues, clubs, and colleges, all that had seemed to be the spontaneous recognition of my book was but the merchandising enterprise of press agents selling a movie. Money and ballyhoo—the fruit of the struggle to write.

Later in the day Josephson came in with a sleek, smiling man in golfing tweeds and a red-and-black-striped tie.

"Miss Yezierska! This is Montague Glass!"

Glass extended a soft plump hand. "I just beat your boss at golf." He laughed. "He paid me off with a copy of *Hungry Hearts*."

I looked at the man who made a living burlesquing Jews for *The Saturday Evening Post*. His face, tanned by the California sun, had the alert eyes of a smart lawyer. He exuded the genial good will of the man on the top of the world.

"I hear your book is a great tear-jerker," he said. "With a few laughs to set off the sob stuff, a story like yours could put you on Easy Street for the rest of your life. It does me good to see some one succeed who deserves success."

I couldn't say a word. There was only the swift clash of antagonism in the air between us. This man, with his beaming kindliness, turned out his caricatures of Jews like sausage meat for the popular weekly and monthly magazines. Americans reading his Potash and Perlmutter stories thought those clowning cloak and suiters were the Jewish people.

After Montague Glass had left, Josephson turned to me with his odd smile. "Goldwyn hired him to do our post-mortem."

"What post-mortem?" I said.

"It's the phrase for doctoring a story. Your story in this case."

"My story?"

"They say *Hungry Hearts* is good as it is but needs
laughs and a happy ending. They think Montague Glass's
name for additional dialogue will be sure to put it over."

I was too horrified to speak.

"You see, Montague Glass has a clever press agent.
This job on *Hungry Hearts* is not only for the money, but
for the advertising his client would get out of it."

"My book is my life," I cried. "I'll not let them murder it with slapstick!"

Josephson's unbeaten calm infuriated me.

"The scenario is as much your work as mine. How can
you let them get away with it?"

"Let them? I can't stop them—and I'm not crazy
enough to try."

"If the boss broke into your house and slept with your
wife, would you also shrug your shoulders?"

He only smiled his odd smile of submissive acceptance.

"Screaming and yelling won't help. You've signed the
contract that they can adapt the story as they think
best. You were lucky that they used as much of your
story as they did."

So this was the price of my sudden riches! For forging
a check, you went to prison. For forging the truth, you
sat with the famous of the hour and as long as the
publicity bolstered you, you'd stay there.

~~~~~~

CHAPTER VIII

A CAT IN THE BAG

THE ENDING of *Hungry Hearts* was out of my hands. My contract with Goldwyn was up, and I had not begun the new story he had asked me to show him. I was too confused, too unsure of myself, to know what to do next.

And then one morning William Fox phoned. He wanted to see me at my earliest convenience.

William Fox was then the spark plug of the movie industry. He had the dramatic flair that could transform a simple small-town girl into Theda Bara, world-famous vamp. He was one of the first producers to attempt realism in his stories. He made the first pictures without artificial happy endings. While the rest of Hollywood still ground out its Pollyanna love stories and Western melodramas, Fox produced the American version of *Les Misérables*. He followed this venture with a still greater success, *Over the Hill*.

I had seen *Over the Hill* a year before reaching Hollywood. The sentimental movie had wrung my emotions. I wept with the crowd over the old couple abandoned by their children, ending their life in the poorhouse. It made me remember how I had abandoned my father and mother. *Over the Hill* showed the parents' tragedy. In the story that I had tried to tell Goldwyn about I wanted to show the loneliness of the children who left their roots, their parents of the Old World.

I had been so convinced that my story was the sequel

83

to *Over the Hill* that I wrote to William Fox. And now, a year later, Fox had sent for me.

A secretary led me through a dim corridor into the lush privacy of the great man's sanctum: dark rich woodwork, stained-glass windows, somber lights, a deep velvet rug, the air was drugged with theatrical mystery.

William Fox walked in. He was a short, thickset, dark-eyed man with an aliveness that made him seem tall and slender.

Like a priest at an altar, he stood at his ornately carved desk and waited for me to sit down.

"It was good of you to come so promptly." Fox smiled, his glance resting on me as if I were already one of his anointed.

"I wanted to talk to you ever since I saw *Over the Hill*," I said. "I saw it three times and each time I wept my heart out."

He leaned toward me, eager to hear what I had to say.

"You've hit on a folk tale, a homespun version of *King Lear*."

"William Fox, the Shakespeare of the movies." He laughed. "That's a good one."

I laughed with him. East Side had met East Side. I looked at the little Hungarian Jew who had started his movie career as the manager of a penny arcade and had raised the industry from pornographic peep shows to some measure of dignity.

I told him that as I had waited in line to buy my ticket to *Over the Hill* an old man, with tears running down his cheeks, had come out of the theater. He stopped near me and smiled. "Take plenty of handkerchiefs—you'll need them."

"We sweated blood for those tears," William Fox confessed happily.

"The story struck a guilty chord in all of us," I said.

"Some critics say I oversentimentalized the mother."

"Then the crowds who flock to see the picture must be sentimentalists too," I said.

"Have you seen my production of *Les Misérables?*"

"I wrote you about it long before I came to Hollywood. . . . You probably never read my letter."

"My secretaries sometimes protect me from the very people I ought to see." He drew his chair closer.

"I walked out of the theater, feeling cheated. . . ."

"Cheated?" He frowned. "Why?"

"I paid fifty cents and gave up two hours of my time to see poverty dressed up in fancy costumes. It was as far from reality as the stories of the working girl in the popular magazines. . . ."

"People go to the movies for escape from real life," he said.

"But your own picture, *Over the Hill,* denies that. You took the poor, the old, those too crushed to hope for a hearing, and made them speak to millions. You can do for pictures what Gorky and Dostoevski did for literature."

"I like your fresh point of view," he said. "We need people with new ideas. I read a synopsis of your book. . . ."

"Only a synopsis?"

"I never have time to read more than a synopsis. Experts do my reading for me."

"Can experts give you the feeling of the original?"

"I'm a busy man." A hard glint came into his eyes. "Selling entertainment to the American public means keeping an eye on the box office before thinking of art. Now, let's get down to business. I want the movie rights of everything you produce in the next three years. I'll give you twenty thousand the first year, thirty thousand the second, and fifty thousand the third."

I stared at him, flattered, frightened. He was offering me a fortune. But was I really a writer?

"I never know from day to day what I can write. . . ."

"I'll take the risk. Writers are a gamble in any case," William Fox said.

"One day I can write—the next day nothing comes. I've got to wait till it comes. I can't force it."

"I know you've got the stuff."

"The trouble with a contract is that it's a contract," I tried to explain.

"Didn't you make a contract for your book?"

"After it was written . . ."

"My contract assures your future. Do you know how I made Mary Carr? I picked her out of a crowd of extras and gave her the lead in *Over the Hill*. I dictated every pose, every move she made. I gave her every bit of her stage business. That woman never knew what she was acting. I didn't want her to know. But I knew what I wanted—what I could make of her. And I know what I can make of you.

"Here's your contract. Take a few days to think it over." He spoke with the compelling force that made people do what he wanted, made hardheaded businessmen invest fabulous sums in his ventures. "Call my secretary for an appointment when you're ready to sign." He pushed back his chair and walked with me to the door.

Back in my hotel I looked at the contract. Twenty thousand dollars, thirty thousand, fifty thousand. Riches! How could I earn all that money working in my slow underground way? I'd have to speed up, cover up with bluff and craftsmanship what I could not create.

To sign or not to sign. To sign and become rich; not to sign and plunge back into poverty. Before coming to Hollywood, a thousand dollars had seemed a million. But now, living at the Miramar Hotel, it was just small change. I'd have to have more and more money to keep up with Hollywood.

Ten thousand dollars hadn't given me happiness or peace of mind, clarity or self-confidence, or knowledge of how to write. But why go back to the old loneliness when working with the wizard of the movies and living at the Miramar Hotel was offered to me?

Was it really an offer? How long would William Fox want me if he discovered that he had picked a cat in a bag? If he found that I had neither genius nor craftsmanship for turning out box-office hits?

In Hollywood the whirling race toward the spotlight, the frantic competition to outdistance the others, the machinery of success had to be kept going. The clock ticked off the minutes, prodding: Produce! Produce! Produce another best seller or get the hell out of here!

I thought of Alice in *Through the Looking Glass.*

"Faster! Faster!" cried the Red Queen, yanking Alice along. *"Now, here, it takes all the running you can do, to keep in the same place."*

I could have returned the unsigned contract by mail, but before going back to loneliness and obscurity, I wanted to take a last look at the theatrical splendor of the William Fox office.

The next afternoon when William Fox smilingly shook hands with me, I became so bewitched by the man I barely managed to take the contract out of my brief case.

"I can't sign," I mumbled, half hoping that he would persuade me to change my mind.

He flashed a puzzled glance. "You're a funny person. I'm giving you the chance of a lifetime. Why can't you sign?"

"Writing is everything I am. . . . It's my search for a meaning. I can't sign it away."

He shook his head, disturbed by the unreasonableness that had no place in his world.

"What is it—honesty or fear or a perverted sense of martyrdom?" He laughed.

"Signing would put me on the spot. I'm not a *professional* writer. I am——"

"Who do you think you are? Joan of Arc, waiting for the voices?"

A turmoil of self-doubt and confusion threatened to engulf me in his laughter.

"I don't know, but I can't sign," I said, placing the contract on his desk.

I walked out, released from the terrible burden of indecision. I looked up at the sky. God! Where do I go from here . . .?

CHAPTER IX

POOR PEOPLE

THE HOLLYWOOD publicity brought me a strange harvest of fan mail. If I had given away my last penny, stripped myself bare, I could not have begun to meet the demand of those letters. People in want of money begged me to remember that I too had known what it was to be hungry and homeless. They felt that I would not be like the heartless rich. I would feel for them. I would help them. Unrecognized geniuses who had written novels or poems that no one would publish reminded me that I had gone about for years with nothing but rejection slips to show for my labor. They wanted me to read their manuscripts and find them a publisher. People with schemes for saving the world asked me to sponsor them. But the greatest number of letters were pleas for money—money—money. I put them aside unanswered, and they haunted me. The weight of all their unsolved problems, their loneliness and need, even their demands for help piled on me a feeling of guilt.

I thought of Charles Garland, a millionaire's son who had appointed a committee to give away his millions to worthy social projects. He preferred the precarious existence of a day laborer to the guilty conscience of a millionaire.

Poor people who had escaped from poverty as I had, feared it, hated it and fled from it all their lives. Those born rich could afford to be touched by it. Kind-hearted rich ladies looked forward to Thanksgiving and Christmas, thrilling days of sight-seeing through the colorful mangers of poverty when they shared with the poor the love in their hearts—brought baskets of fruit to the janitress and the shut-ins at hospital wards. They loved the beggar, the streetwalker, and the convict in prison. For a day they loved to play savior.

I knew of another young millionaire who dreamed of becoming a new St. Francis of Assisi, a brother of the poor on the East Side. His first gesture of renunciation was to leave his father's mansion on Fifth Avenue and become a resident worker at a settlement house. He fell in love with a factory girl, married her, and set up housekeeping in a tenement flat on Hester Street. His banker looked after his coupons while he tried to live the life of those who had nothing.

The story of this saint-inspired millionaire with his dream of brotherhood lent itself to ink and imagination. Newspapers played it up in front-page headlines with such colorful details that even the most cynical veterans of public charity were secretly disturbed lest their front of indifference keep them from a possible windfall. They began to believe in the legend of brotherhood. Didn't the poor always live on hope? Scratch the skin of their incredulity and you exposed their ancestral belief in miracles. Who knew? Maybe the Messiah was about to show Himself in the guise of this brother millionaire. They rushed to him with open arms, ready to share his wealth. All they asked was to unload on his willing shoulders the burden of their poverty. One neighbor was threatened with eviction and needed money for rent. Another needed a lawyer to get young Benny out of a jam. "Brother! I need a pair of shoes." "Brother! I have no shirt on my back." This assault of brotherhood was more than the gentle, saintlike millionaire could take. Stunned and bewildered by the tidal wave of beggars, he barricaded himself and his bride behind locked doors and hired two strong-armed men to keep the poor away.

Even after he fled back to his mansion on Fifth Avenue, the poor pursued him with his dream of brotherhood.

But I was still too close to Hester Street to be able to let my secretary dispose of those letters. They piled up in a huge closet. They overflowed into another, most of them still unread. But when I decided to leave Hollywood, I wanted to silence my conscience by trying to answer some of them.

The first letter I opened was from the Colonial Dames of America:

> We are sure that you, being Polish, will be grateful to this country which has given you so much and eager to contribute to a fund for setting up bronze plaques at every spot where your great countryman, Count Pulaski, trained the Colonial troops during the American Revolution . . .

I dropped the letter into the wastebasket.

The next letter was attached to a large Manila envelope. I began reading in the middle of the page:

> Am I too hopeful in hoping that you will read the poems I enclose? And if you read, will you tell me frankly what you think of them? You who wrote *Hungry Hearts* must sense the hunger of a soul like mine. I hunger for a sign of recognition as you once did. I, too, want to be a writer. I was born in Pittsburgh, the daughter of Polish immigrants. . . .

There followed three more pages of autobiography and a hundred and sixteen lyrics written in longhand.

I picked up another letter, written in a childish hand:

> We have been reading *Hungry Hearts* in class and found it very interesting. Now we have to write a composition about your life. Will you write me something about yourself? My class and I would also very much appreciate if you would send us an autographed picture and a helpful motto for success to frame on our wall in school. . . .

I pushed back the letters, weary as from a hard day's work. I looked at the pile on the floor. A smudged, creased envelope stuck out from the bottom of the heap. There was something foreign in the penciled scrawl. It was dated months ago. I opened the envelope and read: "To the honorable and most respectable Anzia Yezier-ska . . ."

I started to stuff the note back into the envelope, but there was something familiar in the turn of the phrase. The Yiddish of it reminded me of my father. "To the honorable and most respectable:" That was the formal way he used to address a stranger. I picked up the letter again:

Long years and good health on you. May you con-tinue to find in America the land flowing with milk and honey that God in His wisdom did not see fit to let me find.

I read in the *Tageblatt* how you became a new mil-lionaire in Hollywood selling stories from your life as an immigrant. Americans are weighing you in gold for telling them how black you had it in Poland, and how your sun began to shine, coming to America.

To my sad sorrow, mine is a story of an immigrant different from yours. I also came from a village in Poland, like you. But to me, America is a worse *Goluth* than Poland. The ukases and pogroms from the Czar, all the killings that could not kill us, gave us the strength to live with God. Learning was learning—dearer than gold. Poverty was an ornament on a learned man like a red ribbon on a white horse. But here in New York, the synagogues are in the hands of godless lumps of flesh. A butcher, a grocer, any money-maker could buy himself into a president of a synagogue.

With all that was bad under the Czar, the synagogue was still God's light in time of darkness. Better to die there than to live here, among the money-making fat bellies—worshippers of the Golden Calf.

I pray by night and by day, only to go back to my little village in Poland where all know me for what I

am—and will respect me, because I am what I am. I
have nothing left in life but to die. I only want to see
my own before I die. I beg you for a ship ticket to
Poland where I can die and be buried with the honor
Jews give to a man of learning who all his life followed
the footsteps of his fathers.

Do you still remember the sayings from the Torah?
Tzdokeh tatzel bamooves. Charity saves you from death.
The blessings from the next world will be yours for
saving a dying old man from the shame that poverty
and old age has to suffer in America.

From me, honorably and respectfully, your landsman,

BORUCH SHLOMOI MAYER.

The letter had come stamped and dated through the
drab routine of the U. S. mail. But to me it was a voice
out of time, a voice out of eternity, the blowing of the
ram's horn calling Jews to prayer on the Day of Atonement. That homeless old Jew was like a black rock deep
under water, pulling me down into its depth. He called
me back from years of forgetfulness, from the layers of
another life, back to the village in Poland where I was
born. And I remembered the synagogue on the Day of
Atonement. Jews in white shrouds, in the ancestral robes
of death, facing their sins in an ecstasy of abasement
before the throne of Jehovah, chanting the prayer that
was birth, death, and resurrection.

This ancient past that I had despised and rejected with
the ruthlessness of youth now had me by the throat. I
had never really broken away. I had only denied that
which I was in my blood and bones. "Poverty . . . an
ornament . . . like a red ribbon on a white horse. . . ."
Those were my father's words.

I remembered waking up before dawn in our straw-
thatched hut in Poland and seeing Father at his table of
sacred books. His black skullcap setting off his white face
and flaming red beard, his eyes uplifted as he chanted:

"By the rivers of Babylon, there we sat down, yea, we
wept when we remembered Zion . . .

"For they that carried us away captive required of us a song; and they that wasted us required of us mirth, saying, Sing us one of the songs of Zion . . .

"How shall we sing the Lord's song in a strange land . . .?"

We had been hungry, in rags, but the poverty we suffered had been because Father chose to have his portion in the next world. In the depths of our want was glory —pride in Father because he was not like other fathers. He had worked for God as some men work for their wives and children. Poverty had carved his religion on his face.

When we were fleeing from the Czar's pogroms and we had neither bread nor a roof over our heads for the night, Father had but to open the Book of Isaiah: *"Come unto me and hear my song and you shall live."* And we did live. We lived on a song.

When and how had all that we had been so proud of in Poland become something to be ashamed of in America? How had we come to feel that to be poor was a disgrace?

Sitting now with the old Jew's letter before me, I tried to pin down the thing that had caused the change. And then I thought: In America every one tries to better himself, acquire more than he started with, become more important. In a world where all was change, Father alone remained unchanged. He had gone on living his old life, demanding that his children follow his archaic rituals.

And so I had rebelled. I had defied God. Defied heaven in the next world. I wanted life in this world.

My revolt had grown from blind protest into the self-righteous force that charged me to desert Father and Mother because I wanted to cut loose from their strangling hold. I was young. They were old. They had lived their lives. Hadn't I a right to live mine?

And now this old man's plea for a place to die had pulled me back to the dim past, to all those I had abandoned to become a writer. Like a runner who runs a race in a curved track and must get back to his starting point, the distance I had covered running away to live my life with pencil and paper had brought me back to where I had started.

The next day I was on the train to New York. Sitting at the open window, after the train had started, I read the old man's letter again: "Only to go back . . . where all know me for what I am—and will respect me, because I am what I am. . . ."

Here was a self-revealing portrait, a Rembrandt painting of a man rooted in the poetry of his faith. He could sum up the essence of his life in a few simple words. And everything he said shamed me for the ruthlessness of my ambition, the tawdriness of my success. I could not get to Reb Mayer fast enough. I felt as though I had just found my closest kin on earth.

In New York I left my things at the hotel and set out to find him with the zeal of a pilgrim on the way to a holy shrine.

Hester Street roared like a carnival. Above the noise of the rumbling elevated, the clang of trucks and trolleys, the pushcart peddlers shouted their wares. "Bananas! Two for a penny!" "Fresh fish! Only a nickel a pound!" "Potatoes! Last lot cheap!" "Pick them out yourself! Pretzels! Fresh from the oven!" Women with market baskets jammed against each other at the pushcarts, their eyes bright with the zest of bargain hunting, their voices shrill with the fight to get food for their families a penny cheaper.

I had been part of this scene—I had looked on hundreds of times when I was in it. Now I saw it with new eyes. Strange how one can love and hate at the same time. I loved and hated the noise, the dirt, and the foul air from which I had fled. In every bearded old Jew I passed on the street I saw my father—ghosts of the people I had abandoned to "make of myself a person in the world." And now I looked across the gulf, consumed with homesickness and longing for my own kind.

I found the address I sought. It was an old brownstone house with a crumbling stoop wedged between dreary rows of back-to-back tenements. The rusty fire escapes were cluttered with bedding—the rags and patches of poverty. A woman sat on a box nursing her baby and talking to a woman who was dividing a banana between three ragged youngsters. Overhead a woman shook a dust mop.

"Thunder should strike you!" the nursing mother screamed. "Where are you yet? In Minsk?"

"Worms should eat you!" the other yelled back, shaking the dust mop vigorously.

Their brawling merged with the music of a hurdy-gurdy that set the children dancing and shouting with joy. Children everywhere—on the sidewalk, in the gutter, under pushcarts.

As I entered the house, the stench from the toilets in the hall suffocated me. Upstairs, other smells joined in —the smells of cabbage, of herring and onions and the steam of clothes being washed.

A thin, bony woman in a filthy apron answered my knock. She stood in the dark doorway, in an aura of dirt and poverty.

"Does Reb Mayer live here?" I asked.

"Reb Mayer. May his soul rest in peace," she said. "Three months already he is dead."

"Dead?" I stared at her. All those months when I had been killing time in Hollywood, too busy to read my mail, this man had been waiting for an answer to his letter.

"Thank God he's out of this black life." She wagged her head mournfully. Wiping the dust from a chair with the corner of her apron, she asked me to sit down.

I looked about the crowded kitchen. Flies buzzed over the unwashed dishes on the table. Wet stockings and rags hung over the chairs. A bed piled high with mattresses and torn quilts was squeezed between stove and sink.

"His eyes were always up in the sky," she went on. "His head was not on his body, but in the next world.

And just as he started to cross the street a truck knocked him down." Her toothless mouth opened, a dark hole of age and decay. *"Oi weh!"* she sighed. "Such a holy man! And he had to lay there on the sidewalk for hours just like a bum."

She moved aside the dusty curtain of a coffin-like alcove. "This was Reb Mayer's room," she said.

A narrow window looked onto the bottom of a dark chimney-like pit where lay the heaped-up junk of countless years. In the street the sun was shining. Here was the mouldy smell of perpetual night.

A rusty cot, one leg propped up on a soapbox, stood against the wall. A book, face down, was on top of the pile of books on the table. More books were on the window sill. A row of boxes filled with books lined the other wall. On a nail over the cot hung an embroidered velvet bag with the praying shawl and phylacteries. In spite of the cobwebs, the dust, the smells, there was something wonderful about the room. The aura, the *Schina,* of Reb Mayer was still there.

The sacred books, the worn bindings, the moth-eaten velvet bag with the praying shawl on the cobwebbed wall charmed away the squalor of the place. This was the heritage of the uprooted, the mute hymn of the homeless in a strange land.

I picked up the open book and a nest of bedbugs scurried out of the torn binding. One of them ran on my finger and bit me. I dropped the book and brushed the bug away.

"The whole house walks away with the bedbugs," the woman said, offering her apron for me to wipe my hands on. "I wanted to give the books to the synagogue, but when they saw the bugs it was good night! Woe is me! It would be a sin to burn such holy books! And I can't rent the room till the books are out."

She flung out her arms and wailed, *"Gevalt! Gevalt!* I need those books like I need a hole in my head. Reb Mayer could have been a rabbi in a synagogue and eat from the fat of the land by his own table, but a craziness in his head made him go around like a beggar, selling penny shoelaces—dying yet, owing me six months' rent!"

"Here's for the rent," I said, offering her a bill.

Her eyes gloated as she held it up to the light.

"Long years on you, golden heart!" A chuckle rattled out of her throat. "You saved me my life. I can pay now the rent and buy me something for the holidays."

She smoothed out the bill between her bony fingers and kissed it rapturously. "May it be good luck to us all."

I made for the door, but she seized my arm. "Darling *leben*, who are you yet? From where do you come? Tell me only? Are you maybe yet a relation from Reb Mayer?"

"Yes, I am related to Reb Mayer—in a way," I said, pulling away from her.

Then I ran, terrified by the hungry way she grabbed at me, sickened by the smells and the dirt.

Out in the street, I looked back. What had I left behind? I glanced at my purse, my gloves. Everything intact. But still I had a strange, persistent feeling I had left something.

Here were people—ragged, brutal, dirty—crowded into subhuman cubbyholes—without light—without air. Here all the poor of the earth crying for a place in the sun. And all I could feel was disgust—revulsion—escape. Anywhere—only away.

The hotel room was not far enough away. I could not put enough space between me and the squalor, the noise, the smells I had fled. I was more than ever out of step with everything and everybody around me. Often when I looked at myself in the mirror, I saw a strange likeness to that poverty-crushed, bewildered hag. Her eyes followed me about like the eyes of a lost frightened animal. Once you knew what poor people suffered it kept gnawing at you. You'd been there yourself. You wanted to reach out and help. But if you did, you were afraid you might be dragged back into the abyss.

The woman's ravaged face haunted me. I should have

done something for her. But what could I have done?
Those two brown stubs of teeth sticking out of her
shrunken mouth needed a dentist. You had only to look
at a poor person's mouth and you saw the depths of his
poverty. Mother used to say, "Win me only a fortune on
the lottery, and I'll dance myself over to the clinic for
false teeth."

I could have sent that woman to the dentist. But if
I had done that, what about the other toothless women
on the block? And if they had teeth, they should have
something to eat. Give a beggar a dime and he'll bless
you. Give him a dollar and he'll curse you for withholding the rest of your fortune. Poverty is a bag with a hole
at the bottom.

PART TWO

CHAPTER I

ALL WHOM I EVER LOVED

FROM THE wide, sunny windows of my hotel apartment on Fifth Avenue, I could see the Hudson and East Rivers and the skyscrapers of downtown Manhattan. I had been living in my high-towered luxury for three years and still did not feel at home. One Saturday afternoon in June, an overwhelming nostalgia took me back to the East Side. People sprawled about the stoops, leaned out of the windows, the leisure of the Sabbath in their faces.

The rumble of traffic, the feverish jostling and bargain-hunting at the pushcarts were stilled; but from open doorways and windows, radios blared a pandemonium of familiar strains.

On one corner, the water hydrant was turned on to clear the muck from the gutter. Half-naked children in ragged underwear danced and shouted with joy under the shower. In the basement entrance of a tenement sat a white-bearded sage in a black skullcap holding forth to a circle of his neighbors. The sidewalks surged with young folks in their holiday best parading gayly past overflowing garbage cans. They pushed out the walls of their homes to the street on their day of rest.

How often, when I was in Hollywood, had this noisy, crowded ghetto come between me and the parties of "eminent authors." The same dark, irrational compulsion that makes a murderer risk his life to return to the scene of his crime pulled me back to this home that had never

101

been home to me. The very forces that had driven me
away drew me back.

The sunset lit up the sky, splashing the drab tenements
with gold, bringing memories of Sabbath candles and the
smell of *gefüllte* fish. When I had lived on Hester Street,
I would stop at the pushcart of Zalmon Shlomoh, the
hunchbacked fish peddler, to buy his leftover fish for the
Sabbath.

"How goes your luck today?" I used to ask him.

"Except for health and a living, I'm perfectly fine."

He always made the same joke as he wiped his hands
on his sweater gleaming with the scales of the fish. His
broad, bony cheeks, the deformed curve of his back, and
his knotted arthritic hands made him a gnome, a gro-
tesque. But his eyes were alive with the radiance of our
secret code. Except for health and a living, we were both
perfectly fine.

One day he flashed me a look of bold intimacy. *"Und*
how goes it with you? With your red hair, you must be
always on fire!"

Startled, I returned his look. All at once the hunchback became a man in my eyes. It had been a long time
since I had felt so free with any one. I reached out and
touched his arm in responsive gaiety.

"I'm like a sinner in the next world, thrown from one
hell into another."

"But you wouldn't be happy except in hell." Zalmon
laughed back, exposing the black cavities of his yellow
teeth.

That was all I needed to let loose my obsession. "If you
want to know what hell is, I'll tell you. Hell is trying to
do what you can't do, trying to be what you're not——"

"Nu? So what are you trying to be that you're not?"
he bantered.

"It wills itself in me to be a writer——"

"A writer?" He gave me a long, sparkling glance. "A
young girl like you! For what do you need yet to write?"

"Oi weh! I don't know myself." I sighed as he wrapped

the fish in a newspaper and there was no longer any reason to linger at the pushcart. "Time is flying. I can't bear to be left out of life an old maid. Tell me, why do I have to write? When will I live?"

In Zalmon Shlomoh's eyes was such a naked look of comprehension that it silenced me. Unmindful of the hurrying crowd, the shrill cries of the hucksters and the housewives pushing past us with their market baskets, we stood looking at each other. We belonged to the shadowy company of those who were withdrawn from their fellows by grief, illness, or the torment of frustration.

Zalmon turned away and scolded with mock impatience. "You ask more questions in a minute than all the wise men can answer in a lifetime."

He shook his head and gave my arm a wicked little pinch. "God sends always to the spinner his flax, to the drinker his wine, and to a *meshugeneh*, a crazy one like you, an answer to your own *meshugass*. If I weren't old enough to be your father, I'd take you away to the end of the earth where we could both go crazy together; but you deserve a young man your own age. Your red hair and white skin cry out for youth."

"I hate young men! They say I have a *dybbuk*, a devil, a book for a heart. They laugh because I want to be a writer."

Always whenever I saw Zalmon Shlomoh I would feel that I too was a cripple. It leaped out of my eyes like the guilt of secret sin, that devouring hunger in me. People ran away from it as from a deformity. Only Zalmon Shlomoh, the hunchback, could feel and see the wild wolves of that hunger and not be frightened away.

I wondered, as I recalled the days when Zalmon was my only friend, whether he was still alive. If I could reach him, would he be glad to see me? Dared I look him up, to find out? But I knew he could never forgive my becoming one of the bloody rich. I never would look him up.

I thought of the time Zalmon had come to see me with

a newspaper package under his arm. In the secondhand shop he had picked up, for a dime, an old record of Beethoven's "Moonlight Sonata." Instead of talking, he turned on the record again and again, filling the small room with the melancholy tenderness of all the unspoken love in the world.

One night he had taken me to hear Caruso in *Pagliacci*. The grief of the clown reached up to us in the gallery. That glorious voice cried out the ache of our own un-lived lives.

Even while we sat together, cousins in sorrow, I was affronted by Zalmon's fish smells. In his new suit he looked as incongruous as a dog in a praying shawl. His charm was great enough to make me forget the dwarfed deformity of his body, but his fish smells drove me away. I could smell them even now.

They were soaked into me from sweatshop days. When-ever the boss had wanted us to work late without pay, he treated the machine hands to herring and onions. Among themselves the girls grumbled as they bolted the bitter bribe. One night Sara Solomon flared up.

"I got my feller waiting for me on the corner. All I need yet, he should pick himself up another girl——"

"You got to meet your feller?" I said. "*I* got to go to night school. I'm going to be a stenographer——"

"*Nu?* So tell the boss to choke himself with his her-ring——"

"Sure I will!" I grabbed my shawl and stood up. "I don't care if the shop burns down. We sell him our days, but the nights are ours."

Their faces froze. I felt the boss's hand on my neck.

"Out you go! Out of my shop! I want no fresh-mouthed *Amerikanerins!* Greenhorns! The minute they learn a word English, they get flies in their nose and wanna be ladies. I don't want no ladies here!"

A dark period followed the loss of my job. But I had had enough of the sweatshop. I decided I knew enough typing and stenography to look for work in an office. And then I found myself up against a new barrier—the barrier of being a Jew.

A bank in the Jewish clothing district wanted a beginner. I was among the first to apply. The room was crowded with girls when the door of the inner office opened and the personnel manager stuck his head out. "Are there any Jews here?" he asked, briefly scanning the girls' faces. "If so there's no need to stay. No Jewish girls are wanted for this particular job."

I stood up and walked out quickly. Others followed me. Out in the street I could see nothing but that man's face, hear nothing but that man's voice as he said, "No Jewish girls are wanted."

Again and again I was told "No Jews wanted." But I had to have a job and so I kept on answering ads. I could not give up the hope that somewhere in some office it wasn't a crime to be born a Jew. Late at night, as soon as the morning papers were on the stands, I was there studying the Help Wanted columns.

I answered an ad for a stenographer. It was so early I did not expect to find the office open. I walked past the empty switchboard and reception desk, past a row of darkened cubicles. Then I noticed in the far corner a light. A door was open on an inner office where a man was bent over papers on his desk. I was inside the door before he saw me.

He was a big man, in his middle fifties. A great head strongly modeled; the forehead jutted out, throwing his eyes into deep shadow.

"I came about a job," I said. "Can you tell me where to go?"

He glanced at the clock and then back at me. "I didn't expect any one this early——"

"I wanted to be the first to apply," I said.

"Are you a legal stenographer?"

The lines over his high forehead rushed together like sentinels over his gray eyes. Those eyes, sunk deep in their sockets, had a penetrating intelligence that could see through people. I felt he knew I had come to lie my way into the job.

"The ad calls for an experienced stenographer," he reminded me. "What is your experience?"

"Where shall I get experience if no one gives me a chance to get it?" I burst out. "The last place I applied they wouldn't even try me out when I said I was a Jew. Experience! My God! I'm burning up with experience, but not in offices."

He took off his glasses and stared at me. His brows arched and a slow smile spread over his face. "Well, where did you get your experience?"

"In factories—sewing shirts, making artificial flowers, rolling cigars."

"But what I need is an experienced stenographer——"

"Oh, I'm a stenographer, all right! And a good one! I studied in night school——"

Suddenly I realized by the quiet look in his eyes that I was shouting the same way that I bargained at the pushcarts. I flushed with embarrassment and lowered my voice. "Just try me out. I'll show you——"

"All right, show me." He handed me a shorthand pad and pencil. As he dictated I became aware of his voice. It was a kind of voice I had never heard before. The charm of courtesy and kindness was in it and the assurance of education. It was like listening to music that quieted fear.

When I handed him what I had typed, I was afraid it wasn't good enough. For such a man even the typing would have to be somehow superior.

He read it and turned to me. "Young lady, you're hired. When can you start?"

My throat was so dry I had to swallow to get the words out. "You want me? I really have the job?"

"Certainly." He laughed, and then, noticing the anxiety in my face. "What's the matter with you? You've shown me you're capable."

Ashamed of my clumsiness, I said, "I've been turned down so much!"

He stood up, stretched his arms, and I saw how tall he was. "Look here," he said casually, "I've been working all night in this office. I'm going for breakfast. Would you like a cup of coffee?"

I gaped at him. Such friendliness from a boss!

"Come on! Let's go!" He opened the door. And suddenly all strangeness between us was gone.

"It's so wonderful to have a job in an office!" I told him. "After what I've been through to be hired—by a person like you—a real American."

His smile showed he liked being appreciated. There were bright pin points of light in his eyes—flecks of sunlight on gray water.

In the restaurant, I spread out the napkin, touched the tablecloth, drank the coffee. Real, I kept telling myself, looking at everything around me but not at him.

"When I put the ad in the *Times* I did not expect to find any one like you," he said. "You are a very unusual person."

He patted my hand. It was a gesture of simple kindness, but it stirred currents in me that had never before been touched. The mountain of hurts I carried on my back from czarist Russia, and the hurts piled up looking for a job in America, dissolved. I had been accepted, recognized as a person. . . . I tasted the bread and wine of equality.

Morrow's office was on the twentieth floor of a Wall Street skyscraper. The sunlight, the air. the view all around New York introduced me to a life outside all my experience. I looked out of the clean windows and saw the grimy, barred windows of Cohen's Shirt Factory. I pitied the people I had left behind in the noisy clatter of the machines.

My desk was just outside Morrow's office. The switchboard and reception desk screened outsiders from us, and we were also removed from the rest of the floor where his assistants worked.

There had always been a chasm between earning my living and living my life. Earning a living had meant drudgery, the chain around my neck—until I worked for John Morrow. Working with him, I was learning and growing every day.

Once, when there was some overtime work, he asked me to dine with him. "My family is out of town and I hate eating alone," he said.

He asked me to take him to an East Side restaurant and we went to Yoneh Shimmel's on Delancey Street.

After dinner we walked through lines of pushcarts to Allen Street, where the basement shops showed brass samovars, old shawls, and trays from Palestine.

"This is like a foreign country!" he said, marveling.

After that staying late for a job was like a holiday, because it meant dining with him when the work was finished.

I had to prove to him that he had made no mistake in choosing an awkward girl from Hester Street instead of the lady-like college secretary he could have had. All I had to offer was the manuscript about the people in the sweatshop. As he was getting ready to go home one afternoon I stuck it into his coat pocket and asked him to read it.

The first thing he said when he came in the following morning was, "I've read it! I've read it! That sweatshop is shocking, terrifying! And you've survived it. You've risen out of it!"

He seemed to be very much moved, and that was all he said. But all that morning I was conscious of his eyes on me. No other man had ever looked at me like that.

Later in the afternoon he came over to me, put the manuscript on my desk. "This is rough now, but alive." His hand touched mine, withdrew instantly. In that brief touch all the unlived in me leaped into life.

I had found some one who saw me, knew me, reassured me that I existed. And writing ceased to have the desperate urgency it used to have. The greatest words ever written were pale and thin beside the new life I was living.

We dined often on the East Side. At first I had been embarrassed about showing him the dirty streets, the haggling and bargaining, and the smells from the alleys of the ghetto where I lived. But what I had thought coarse and commonplace was to him exotic. My Old World was so fresh and new to him it became fresh and new to me.

Sometimes we went to the Yiddish theater. Leaving the theater one night, he stopped to buy baked sweet potatoes from a pushcart peddler, and we ate them as we walked along.

"I thought I'd become a lady working for you," I laughed. "And now you're dragging me down to eating from pushcarts."

He looked into my eyes, and his look burned through me. I was suspended in the concentration of his gaze. "You don't have to become. You suffer from striving. You try to be. But you are, you are already."

There were always pauses in the midst of our work for our private conversations. One afternoon we were talking about a Yiddish play we had seen the evening before. It surprised me how well he understood everything without knowing Yiddish. He said the emotion of the actors was so vivid and the audience so responsive that this interested him more than the play.

"You know, they have something you have too," he said, studying me. "The same intensity. I think it comes from fighting for every inch of ground on which you stand——"

"My fight has been only to keep alive," I protested. "You're a fighter, too, but for others——"

"Oh, my dear." He shook his head. "I've never fought for anything with the spirit that you have. I like the passion with which you live every moment. Everything that has ever happened to you is in your eyes."

The ringing of the telephone interrupted us. I answered

it, and then told him that Mrs. Morrow was in the reception room.

He flushed and turned back to his desk. "Ask her to come in," he said.

Mrs. Morrow, a gracious woman in her fifties with an intelligent, attractive face, smiled at me as she entered. It was the first time I had ever seen her, and I felt instantly that she was everything I was not.

The delicate perfume, the slender elegance of her shoes, the softly tailored gray suit, the perfection of her shining gray hair were details of a rich life I had only read about. She had a natural poise and elegance. She was kind with the kindness of one whose position in the world was secure.

Her visit was brief. She had called to drive her husband home. They left the office together.

I went home alone. I was aware for the rest of the evening how far from me he was, how unpossessable. He had withdrawn into a world of culture and beautiful living where I could never enter.

But I consoled myself. I knew him as neither his wife nor children could know him. They had his name, his money, his reputation, but I had something that fed his spirit. He could never share with his family the thoughts he shared with me. Our need for each other burned away the differences between Gentile and Jew, native and immigrant—the barriers of race, class, and education.

In my dreams I felt myself more married to him than his wife, closer to him than his children.

I was twenty-three. I had never loved any one before. On the East Side there was no privacy, couples seized their chance to be together wherever they found it; they embraced in hallways, lay together on roofs. I had passed them all with eyes averted.

My love needed a sanctuary, a solitude of sky and stars. Away from work, away from him, I walked Brooklyn Bridge night after night, recreating my every experience with him: the way he looked at me, the words he said, trying to hold close the golden moments of being understood.

He stayed more often in the office after the others were gone, just to talk. He would walk me home. He lingered at the door of my house, reluctant to end the evening. We could never finish all we had to say.

Then one day he had to go to Chicago on business. As I helped him pack his portfolio, we avoided looking at each other. When it was time to go, he mumbled good-by and hurried out, without a glance at me. A moment later he returned, made his way to his desk and began opening and shutting drawers.

"Have you forgotten something?" I asked.

He looked up. "Hell! I'll be late for my train. I'll write." And he was gone.

I counted the hours it would take him to get to Chicago. Would he write on the train or when he arrived? How long would it take for his letter to reach me? I met the mailman impatiently twice a day.

When at last his letter came I ripped it open and read:

> I had so much to say to you before I left, but I was tongue-tied. I fear I'm still too inhibited to say what I want to say.
>
> My life has been an evasion of life. I substituted reason for emotion, hiding behind a shell of safe abstractions. I've been so repressed by the fear of feeling, now when I want to tell you what I feel, I'm dumb —I can't get the words out.

And on a separate sheet were these lines:

> I arise from a long, long night of thoughtless
>   dreams,
> Joyless, griefless begins the web of unillumined
>   duties,
> A silken web in which I'm bound.
>   Earthward my eyes,
> Lest your spirit keep me from the pact with my
>   possessions

And lure me to your wilderness of tears,
Where no harvest shall I reap, save stabs and
     flames of pain
 And wan exhaustion, among the unshepherded
     sheep of thought
Who travel through trackless wilds of untamed
     desire.

Day after day more letters came. Each was a freer
avowal of his love.

I never knew how starved I was until I met you. I
was sunk inside my little world of business and family
front, petrified by the inertia of abundance. You saved
me from the barren existence of eat, sleep, and mul-
tiply. I must begin humbly, like a child, to learn the
meaning of life from you. Without you I'm the dry
dust of hopes unrealized. You are fire, water, sunshine
and desire.

Those letters seemed to me the greatest literature I
had ever read. Shelley's odes and Shakespeare's sonnets
had made famous pages in the world's books. But Morrow's words were written for me.

One evening I sat in the office after the others were
gone. I had put on my hat and coat, and as I closed my
desk I thought of the words of his letter: "Dear love
of God! All whom I ever loved I love in you. . . . Your
father, your brother, your son, your lover . . ."

Suddenly he was standing in the doorway. I wondered
if thinking of him had made him appear. I thought if
ever God was visible in a human face it was here, in him.

"Come!" he said, taking my arm. "I want to talk to
you."

For a time we walked without looking at each other,
without touching. In his last letter he had written: "Now
is our moment. Our moment is our only eternity."

I remembered an old ghetto saying: "Throw me in fire
and water, but throw me among my own." Those words
had a new meaning for me now. John Morrow was more

my own than my mother and father. If I had never met him I would have dreamed him into being.

Instinctively, as if he read my thoughts, he took my hand in his, caressing the palm. He interlocked his fingers with mine. And so we walked till we found ourselves at the pier under Williamsburg Bridge. Behind us were the black silhouettes of factories and tenements. Before us the deep, dark river. The current seemed to pull us down into its drowning depths.

"I never learned to swim," I said. "The river fills me with terror."

"Don't be afraid," he whispered.

For a long moment we stood silent. Then I was in his arms and he was kissing me. His hand touched my breast. The natural delight of his touch was checked by a wild alarm that stiffened me with fear. I had the same fear of drowning in his arms that I had of drowning in the river. His overwhelming nearness, the tense body closing in on me was pushing us apart instead of fusing us. A dark river of distrust rose between us. I had not dreamed that God could become flesh.

Sensing my unyielding body, he released me.

Our walk home was an agony of confusion. Old fears bred into me before I was born, taboos older than my father's memory, conflicts between the things I had learned and those I could not forget held me rigid.

At the door I was torn between asking him up to my room and the fear that if I gave myself to him I'd hate him. And if I didn't, I'd lose him. He settled it by kissing me good night and walking away.

The moment he turned the corner I wanted to run after him and beg him to come home with me. But instead I stumbled slowly back to my room.

CHAPTER II

END OF A DREAM

THE NEXT morning I walked into his office and he did not look up. He was bent over his desk. His face was expressionless. Overnight his warm, outgoing intimacy had turned into the petrified indifference of a stranger.

I stood waiting, terrified by his coldness.

In a voice strange and faraway he said, "Go to the Supreme Court, copy the record of the Roberts case, and make an extract of Kober's testimony." And still without looking at me, he went on with his work.

I had been up all night reliving the moment in his arms, torn with regret for the blind fears that had driven me from him when I wanted him most. Now I was awakened, fully responsive, ready to throw myself at his feet with all the abandon of first love. And he was sending me away to copy an old record of a law case.

Had he too been up all night? Had he decided it was impossible to begin a new life with an immature girl of twenty-three?

There was something pitiless and inhuman in his averted face. What had I done to have turned fire into ice?

The man who had opened the door to a new life had slammed that door in my face. The man who had awakened poetry and dreams had suddenly become a preoccupied attorney.

When I returned in the late afternoon, I found a note

114

on my desk telling me not to come to the office next morning, but to go directly to the court and work there till the record was completed.

Two days later, I found a new girl in the office.

"Too much work for you to do alone," he said. "I want you to clear up the files. They're too cluttered."

Weariness lay like fine dust in the pallor of his face. Submerged though I was in my own grief, I sensed his leaden fatigue. For the first time I saw he had grown old.

I wanted to cry out to him: "I'm older than you. I was born old. I love your tiredness, your oldness with a love that youth can never know." But the cry remained locked in my throat.

I kept at those files day after day while I watched the other girl take dictation and do all the personal things that had once belonged to me.

By extraordinary self-control, I managed to clean up the files. And then he set me to copying complicated financial reports. Hour after hour, day after day, I copied figures. He ignored me so completely my very existence ceased. I had become part of the office furniture, an automaton for carrying out office routine.

One day the other girl became ill and had to go home. As soon as she was out of the room, I rushed to his desk.

"I must talk to you," I said.

He frowned, avoiding my eyes. "Not now."

"Now! Now!" I pounded his desk. "Now I must talk to you——"

"There's nothing more to talk about," he said.

"What have I done?" I flung myself against the stone wall that he put up. "Why are you so different?"

"I'm sorry we're so busy, but work has piled up. Two new, difficult cases——"

"But you don't let me help you any more. I'm just copying. There's a limit to human endurance of drudgery——"

"Some one has to do the drudgery. If—if you don't like it here, maybe you ought to look for another job."

His eyelids dropped, and his face, undefended by his

eyes, lay open to my gaze. I was appalled at its sadness.

"You have a great capacity for unhappiness," he said.

"My unhappiness is only loving you."

Harsh lines rose between his brows. "You want love, but you do not want me. You do not love me. You only dramatize your want of love——"

"You're all that I want in life. You've given me myself."

His eyes softened and he bent toward me. "Some day when you're older, you'll see I have nothing more to give you. I've given you everything I had. I'm an old man and you're only twenty-three. The years ahead of me are short, leading to the end. And yours are long, leading to the beginning of life."

His words silenced me for a moment, and I said sadly, "All that I feel is that you loved me. And suddenly you hate me. You kill me with coldness." Then I turned to him in all my terrible egoism. "Tell me, do you hate me because I break up your safe, sheltered life?"

His jaw set with a click. He put on dignity as if it were a cloak and leveled at me a cold, hard stare I would never forget.

"You're an emotional, hysterical girl, and you have exaggerated my friendly interest."

My eyes burned into his eyes till he was forced to look at me.

"Why did you write me those letters? If your letters lie, then there is no truth in this world."

"Oh, my letters! I think you had better return them now."

There was a pleading unsure note in his voice for the first time. I saw with horror that fear was all that was left of his love. I began to babble without knowing what I said. When I heard my own voice with a shock of surprise, I could neither control my words nor stop saying them.

"Your letters are mine. Mine! Mine! You'll never get

them. You don't give a damn what happens to me. All you care is to be safe. Safe with your wife and children. Well, you can have your safety. I'll have your letters."

A spot of color shone on his pale face, but when he spoke, his voice had the quiet patience of a man accustomed to dealing with criminals and maniacs.

"Sit down. Compose yourself."

In my anger I fled to the door and slammed it behind me.

I walked away, telling myself it was all over. Over? A storm of emotion swept away reason; it had only begun!

Wherever I went, the street, the subway, in every crowd, I looked for him, thinking what I would say. I composed countless monologues and tried them out on the deaf and dumb air: Deny me, destroy me, but I love you. I have no existence without you. . . . When you befriended me, I breathed the air of the high places where love comes from, and I can't go back to the old life. . . .

But all my entreaties scattered to the winds at the rankling memory of his last words: "You do not love me. You only dramatize your want of love."

Was it possible? Could it be true that my love wasn't love, my suffering only acting? Was pain unreal? I felt I was falling, falling into a dark, soundless canyon, plunging into lower depths of loneliness than any I had ever known. My life cracked. Everything was tearing open and splitting apart.

In this abysmal loneliness, I clung to the memory of his voice, his eyes, when he loved me. I read and reread his letters. The more I read them, the more I believed he still loved me. I had only to read the first words of his letter: "Dear love of God!" and doubt vanished, the bleak years of loneliness dissolved, life lay open in all directions, all that I lacked was mine. I had to write what love meant to me. But words could not get hold of what I wanted to say. Pages upon pages piled on my table, formless, inchoate. . . . When I walked the streets, the people I passed were shadows.

"*Gevalt!*" Zalmon Shlomoh stopped me one day. "What's with you the matter?" He wiped his hands on his sweater gleaming with the scales from the fish. Then he pulled out a stool from under his pushcart and made me sit down. "*Nu?* So tell me, what's eating you out your heart now that you don't see nobody?"

Startled, I looked at him, and I saw myself as in a mirror. I saw my own hump of inferiority. Here was life, right here on my own block, in the house where I lived, and I cried for the moon. Hannah Breineh, the janitress, cursing and shrieking at the children she loved till they fled from her in hate. The old Jew, sitting on the sidewalk, discussing the cabala with his cronies, his eyes on the stars and his feet in the gutter. That moment I saw a little bit of what I was trying to understand. In all of them I saw a part of myself.

When I returned to my room, I pushed aside the unfinished pages to Morrow, and I started to write about Zalmon Shlomoh, Hannah Breineh, and the old Jew.

The writing became an absorbing, growing thing. It fed and devoured me. It blotted out nights and days until I plucked out of the contradictions of a human being the living seed of a story.

For years those stories went begging, fighting through mountains of rejection slips until one startling day, instead of the usual printed form, there was a letter, and a check, from *Century Magazine.* Then *Harper's, Scribner's, Metropolitan, New Republic.* My greatest joy when a story got into print was to send it to John Morrow. He never acknowledged them, yet I kept sending him a copy of everything I wrote.

One day in my long self-imprisonment the door of my lonely room burst open. Edward O'Brien, the first anthologist of "best" short stories, announced that mine was the best of the best that year.

Overnight people came, magazine editors and book

publishers, asking for more. In the intoxication of this sudden recognition, all my hunger and longing for love turned to ambition. I saw a place for myself. I saw work. I, the unwanted one, was wanted. If I could not have love, I would have fame, success.

~~~~~~

CHAPTER III

A WOMAN OF LETTERS

EVER SINCE Hollywood I had fought back the fear that I was not really a writer. The fabulous sums I was being paid for anything to which I signed my name could not convince me.

I looked about my living room flooded with sunshine. For once I had treated myself to the fine expensive things I had always wanted. I had spent a lot of time and money choosing the furnishings that had transformed the over-stuffed hotel apartment into its present austerity. The bare, unpainted floor, scrubbed to show the grain of the wood, pale-gray walls, plain unpainted furniture: a desk, a chair, an open bookshelf, a low couch covered with monk's cloth. There was an air of coolness and aloneness about the room. Except for the flowers, it might have been a nun's cell.

To make writing easier, I had reduced my life to the simplest essentials. At the lift of the telephone a maid cleaned my place, a waiter brought in food, a bellboy did all my errands.

When I had lived in dingy furnished rooms and worn pushcart clothes, I had dreamed of this beautiful room, this plain costly dress I wore, as part of the simplicity I longed for in my writing. But now—after many years and much labor—I had acquired this beautiful simplicity, and I was struck dumb. I could buy everything I wanted except the driving force I once had to inspire my work.

Bitterly I told myself that I had never found any one

among the literati as real as Zalmon, the fish peddler,
or Sopkin, the butcher, or Hannah Breineh, haggling at
the pushcarts over a penny. But now they no longer came
to see me as friends but only as beggars. They envied
and despised me as I had once envied and despised those
who had what I wanted.

I saw them shaking a warning finger at me with the
old ghetto saying: "Can fire and water be together?
Neither can godliness and ease."

To escape these black thoughts, I searched my files for
the story Frank Crane had written about me six years
before. That was when I had thought success was all the
world had said it was. And Crane, a Hearst columnist,
had handed it to me with this one tabloid sermonette. I
started to read it in the middle of the page:

> Here was an East Side Jewess who had struggled and
> suffered the desperate battle for life amid the swarms
> of New York. She had lived on next to nothing at
> times. She had hungered and shivered and endured.
> Why? Because she wanted to write. And that, ladies
> and gentlemen, is all there is to genius. An undying
> flame, an unconquerable hope, an inviolable belief that
> you are God's stenographer.
>
> Most people do not want too much. They do not
> know what they want. To want anything from the
> hairs of your head to your toenails, with every pulse
> of your blood and every breath of your spirit, to want
> it, waking or dreaming, year in and year out, to burn
> up in it your family, your clothes, your food, your
> reputation, and then leap soul foremost into the furnace
> yourself—when anybody wants like that, let lesser men
> make way. . . .
>
> From a sweatshop worker to a famous writer! All
> because she dipped her pen in her heart . . .

That column was colorful journalism; it had sold *Hungry Hearts* to the movies. But now, six years later, the
overlavish praise nauseated me.

The publicity for each new book had repeated the

Cinderella rise from rags to riches. But it was a stale story now. I had written myself out. I could drive myself no longer. Now I had to face the fact that the books published after *Hungry Hearts,* instead of getting better, were becoming thinner and thinner.

I looked at the page in my typewriter. Words without fire, without life; words forced out of me to hide my dead heart. In sudden disgust I wanted to tear the page. The telephone rang.

It was Professor William Lyon Phelps. "Can you lunch with me? I'm going to be in your neighborhood this morning."

His voice was a last-minute reprieve. I was lifted out of my gloom into a cloud of happiness at the thought of being seen with some one so important in the literary world.

"I'd be delighted," I said, hoping he could not detect the excitement in my voice.

I had lunched with him several times at the Yale Club, dined and gone to the theater with him occasionally, but always by appointment made days in advance. This casual call made me feel that his interest in my work was becoming friendship.

I hurried into my most extravagant costume, a peasant dress of soft blue wool with a white collar made by Valentina. By the time Phelps arrived, I was dressed for a literary flirtation.

He brought with him the odor of eau de cologne and Corona Corona, the air of a man who lived the good life and found it charming and comfortable. His patrician face glowed with benevolence. He was a god dispensing the nectar of his approval to mortals.

"Nice place you have here." He glanced about my room. "Why don't more people unclutter their apartments?"

"Oh, it's just a workshop," I said.

"And what's this you're wearing?" He held me at arms' length. "Your simplicity is the essence of taste."

I looked at this man of ease and thought how I had labored to contrive my simplicity.

Going down in the elevator, he told me that he had just come from Rebecca West, who was visiting New York. Famous names fell from his lips as he talked and he made me feel one of them. His "As I Like It" column had for me the fascination of going backstage where literature was being made. Often I had read, in his news about town, some of my own comments on the plays we had seen together, and I always felt flattered at being quoted by the literary popularizer of the day.

When we entered the Algonquin dining room, eyes turned toward us. Woollcott, Parker, Benchley, Broun, all the current literary cliques, were there—and as we walked to our place, the hum of conversation resumed. At the adjoining table Glenn Frank stood up for a moment to say hello.

The waiter brought us martinis. I glanced at Phelps's cameo face, his smooth, closely shaven skin, his well-brushed hair, slightly gray at the temples.

"How do you always manage to look so perfect?" I asked.

"Perfect? What do you mean?" His pleased smile drew me on.

"All of you is so terribly correct. How do you do it?"

"I didn't realize I was such a paragon."

"Do you remember that time at Town Hall? You had to change your clothes before going to lunch because you had perspired so much while you delivered your lecture. I was flabbergasted. Good God! Professor William Lyon Phelps, Beau Brummell of Yale University, wet with sweat like any ordinary man——"

"Really?" His eyes twinkled as he twirled his glass. "Is that what you think?"

"You're so utterly beyond the sweat of struggle. Your voice flows so evenly when you talk. On the lecture platform, you look so cold in the heart and clear in the head."

Little lines of laughter curled around his eyes, spread

over his entire face. "Cold in the heart and clear in the head." He patted my hand. "Certainly not now."

He took out a galley proof from his pocket.

"Here, my dear, I have something to show you."

It was the proof of a Phelps's feature for the *International Book Review*.

I read the title out loud: " 'The Heroine as a Woman of Letters.' "

"It's about you," he said as I started to read.

If I had one thousandth part of the ability in English composition possessed by the late Thomas Carlyle, I should like to add an appendix to his printed lectures, and call it, "The Heroine as a Woman of Letters." Anzia Yezierska entered this country with no knowledge of English, and no education in her native tongue; her determination to become an American novelist seemed at the time as practicable as if she had determined to have three terms in the White House. But by working in sweatshops and other forms of drudgery all day, and by studying English all night, that is, by sacrificing sleep, food, clothing, shelter and health, she is now a distinguished American novelist, a woman of letters. The oft-told story cannot be too often repeated; at one time in her fight for a livelihood, she went to a famous New York hotel to get a job at scrubbing or as a scullion; her clothes and general appearance caused her rejection. Not many years after this unsuccessful venture, she went to the same hotel as a guest of honor at a literary banquet.

Well I remembered that literary banquet! It had been a publicity stunt—Hollywood style. I happened to tell Horace Liveright, my publisher, that I had once applied for work as a chambermaid at the Waldorf Astoria and couldn't qualify. With his flair for the sensational, Liveright had deliberately staged a banquet there to boost the sale of my new book *Salome of the Tenements*. And Professor Phelps, in his talk at the banquet, had endowed the advertising stunt with literary significance.

I read on avidly:

She writes about life, not as a reporter, social student, slummer or reformer, but as one who has lived it before describing it. . . . She has, in one sense of the word, no literary style. There was so much style in some of Meredith and Henry James that it got between the reader and the object. In the works of Tolstoy, the style is like plate glass, so perfectly does the plain, simple word fit the thought, but in Anzia Yezierska's tales there is nothing. One does not seem to read, one is too completely inside.

A woman of letters!—If I was a woman of letters, I was no fraud. If a college professor, a national authority on literature, praised my style, then I must be a writer!

But the scullion from Hester Street protested: You've been writing with your eye over your shoulder, so dazzled by a little tawdry praise you've lost the meaning of what you had to write. There's no swindler like a snob, a self-swindler.

"It's wonderful!" I said aloud to Phelps. "You're terribly good to me."

Frank Crane came over, and noticing the proof in my hand, asked, "What's this?" I let him read it. When he finished he put his arm around my shoulder.

"This is my girl." He beamed at me. "I discovered her first."

He took my hand and held it as he talked. "My editorial made her known to millions."

Overhearing the conversation, Glenn Frank leaned over, protesting, "Don't forget I published her first story——"

"Yes, indeed, and after every other editor in the country had rejected it," I said.

"I know a couple of others who claim to be her discoverers." Phelps laughed. And then turning to me: "Well, only seven cities claim to be the birthplace of Homer. See how many editors have staked a claim on you!"

An unreasoning rage flared up in me at their laughter. Just what were they so cheerful about? Were they glad because I had been discovered, or because they had discovered me?

Never before had I had the courage to look them in the face and see them as ordinary human beings. I had been awed by their power to damn or praise. What a lucky break, I had thought, to have these arbiters of literature my friends! But now their pride in me, their possessive solicitude roused the rage of a Cinderella against the powers that could cast her back to the ash heap.

I studied Glenn Frank with newly opened eyes. He was his own syndicated column, "Life's Worth Living," in expensively clothed flesh. His smile showed how well pleased he was with the comfortable place he had made for himself.

He and the other literary pontiffs were promoters, talent scouts for the book trade. Their business was booming best sellers. I was their find as long as I reflected glory on them. As long as I was a rising star, I was in their orbit and it was their business to make a fuss over me. At my first flop their blurbs would go on the next best seller.

And Professor Phelps, the literary dictator of America, he was always just coming or going from the great or near great. A hummingbird who flitted from celebrity to celebrity, gathering tidbits for his *As I Like It*.

But with Frank Crane, my anger dwindled. He was a kindly old man who enjoyed being popular and didn't try too hard to question why. The fact that he was a former preacher enabled him to demonstrate in his own life that a camel can pass through the eye of a needle.

They were talking to me and I was answering them brightly, as if I felt the greatest joy in their presence, all the while my thoughts raced on.

Phelps's voice came to me from afar: "I've included your *Hungry Hearts* in my lecture on the best books of recent years——"

"That assures me of immortality," I laughed. But I went on thinking. Next year would I still be among his best authors?

I felt a queer kind of triumph, visualizing my downfall

when my boosters would discover that I was neither the genius nor the woman of letters they had said I was.

"I have good news for you." Frank Crane turned to me. "I've just come back from a lecture at Ohio State University and I heard the journalism sorority is inviting you to address their annual meeting. . . ."

"But I'm no speaker. I die of fright when I face an audience——"

"You don't have to say much," Crane said. "All they want is to see you."

"It's good business for an author to appear in public," Phelps said. "It boosts the sale of books."

I was silent. Who was I to speak out against the gospel of the cash register? In my lust for recognition I had cheated, denied and duped myself for so long, I no longer had the integrity to say what I believed.

Back in my apartment, I reread the page still in my typewriter. It was as false as the talk at the luncheon I had just come from. Every labored word lacked the ring of truth.

I felt myself banished forever from the happy, sleep-walking existence of every one else. I had lost the human ties and emotions that sustained others. Without a country, without a people, I could live only in a world I had created out of my brain. I could not live unless I wrote. And I could not write any more. I had gone too far away from life, and I did not know how to get back.

Once before I had been lost. An immigrant, jobless, friendless, cast out from the sweatshop because I rebelled against nightwork without pay. And then the miracle! John Morrow! The intoxication of being treated like a human being for the first time in my life! He was the only man who knew me as God knows us.

Indelible lines he had written for me etched themselves into my very brain. "You should not suffer as if you are dumb and stifled. You are beautifully communicative in simply being yourself. . . . You do not have to strive, or try to achieve, or accomplish. You are already. I repeat it to you a million times, dear heart. All things of the spirit are yours, now. . . ."

It had been years since I had read his letters. I had deliberately shut out the memory of them. But now the longing to read them again came over me. I needed to reassure myself that this great beauty and goodness had once touched me—for all time.

The box had gathered dust on the shelf. With reverent fingers, I lifted the lid and paused to still the pounding of my heart. I opened the top letter.

"Dear love of God!" I read. And then his stony, dead face on the last day I saw him came between me and the yellowed page. "You're an emotional, hysterical girl and have exaggerated my friendly interest."

How blind! How infatuated I had been! All those days while I had gone around heartbroken, mutely imploring him to notice me, he must have been thankful to be back in his normal routine. The sight of me must have been a constant irritation and reminder of his folly: I had been part of a midsummer's dream in which he had been wearing the ass's head.

"Dear love of God!" I tried to read on. No use. It was a tomb I had opened. I looked at what had once been a loved face, disintegrated beyond recognition. Nothing had survived.

I ripped the letter in half. One after another, I tore the letters, threw them into the fireplace. I struck a match, tossed it into the pile and watched the flame turn to ashes words that had once been to me music, poetry, and religion.

In the morning the letter came from Ohio State University, asking me to address the journalism sorority. I accepted with alacrity.

~~~~~~

CHAPTER IV

MY LAST HOLLYWOOD SCRIPT

I STOOD in a huge hall, between the president of the university and the president of the sorority, shaking hands. An endless double line of faces smiled up at me, hands reached out to clasp my hand. The gleaming lights of the great hall dazzled me, and still more dazzling were the young girls dressed as if for a ball in low-necked evening gowns. The blue wool dress I wore looked like sackcloth against the colorful chiffons and silks of my audience.

I thought of the days when I had watched from the side lines of a theater. Those gowns had always been to me the symbol of another world. I had never had an evening gown. Now that I could afford to buy one, I felt I was too old to wear it.

A wave of self-pity drowned out my stage fright. I wanted to bury my face in my hands and weep because I had never been young and beautiful like the girls who were coming up now to shake my hand.

I looked at these lovely creatures floating on the surface of life. The joy of youth glowed in their faces. Homes sheltered them from what went on in the world. They were born into the good things of life—education, clothes, friends. The give and take of love was as natural to them as breathing.

The room sang with their gay young voices until the signal came to file into the banquet hall. With the solemnity of a ritual, the president led me to my place at the center table. An elaborate dinner was served, but I could not eat. I kept glancing at the notes in my hand, rehearsing my speech. I had learned it by heart, but the words were slipping away, my mind turning blank. What a fool I was to have come here, only to expose my ignorance, my terror of strangers!

All at once I became aware of eyes. Hungry young eyes boring into me. Eyes filled with blind faith, crying for miracles. Eyes like X-rays peering into me to discover the formula for quick success, the touchstone for becoming famous overnight. Eyes, all prayer and pleading: How can we conquer the world? Tell us your secret.

These lucky young girls—envying me! They didn't even know how happy they were. Everything the world could give was theirs—and yet they wanted something from me! What had I to give them? Hunger? Homelessness? The brutal fight to make my way?

Suddenly I hated them. They, who had everything, now wanted to wrest from me they knew not what. I'd give it to them. I'd give them a whiff of Hester Street.

Without waiting for the chairman to introduce me, I stood up and plunged right in. "I have here, in my hands, the few words I had prepared to say to you. It was written before I looked into your eyes. There's something in your eyes that tells me you don't want speeches. You don't want the fairy tale, the success story of the movies. You deserve the truth.

"I feel as if I had started writing a story and then had to scrap everything I had written. Your eyes are giving me courage to tell you the truth."

Such swift response rushed to me out of their eyes! I felt like a parent, arm upraised to strike an errant child —shamed by the wide, trusting look of innocence. Something opened between us that made me talk as if I had always known them. In the past whenever I spoke to an audience, my voice had sounded like a ventriloquist's dummy. But now my voice flowed with an ease I had never experienced.

"What is your conception of success? My idea of success is to be wholly myself. I was always afraid to be myself. This is the first time I have faced an audience without fear.

"Look! I'm tearing up my prepared speech—my last Hollywood script." I tossed the pieces into the air like a bunch of confetti. "Isn't it wonderful—just to be yourself! And you can only be yourself when among friends. We're just people, drawn to one another at sight, swapping experiences. Write out any questions you want to ask me on the back of your menu cards."

And so while dinner was served, the questions were passed up to me. It was such a relief to have said those few words I could even swallow a few sips of soup before I stood up again to read aloud the first question: *What helped you most to become a writer?*

"My greatest stimulus to writing was the teacher who said, 'There are too many writers and too few cooks,' and advised me to stick to the job that assured me a living. I told him if I had to spend my life cooking for a living, that would be existing, not living.

"He said to me, 'Even if you learned to write what you want to write, who would read it? Where would you sell it? There's no market for your stuff. People aren't interested in the immigrant, in poverty, in suffering. They want to be entertained. They need cheering up. Your stuff lacks humor. It's too full of gloom. People read to escape from their troubles. They want glamour, romance. Read the popular magazines. Read what successful authors are writing.'

" 'But why should I copy other authors when I have something of my own to write?' I asked him.

"It was his practical formula for popular magazine success which drove me to defy all sound advice—all reason and common sense—to forsake family, friends, do without sleep, without clothes, withdraw from the world, from life itself—to write. But it was not long before I discovered that a writer cannot withdraw from life and go on writing, any more than a candle can burn without oxygen."

There were many such questions that I answered briefly, but one was a challenge that took up most of the evening. *"You said in a newspaper interview that the things which could not kill you were the making of you. What things did you mean?"*

"There were so many things that crushed the life out of me, so many ways of dying. Every step of the way up in my writing career was enough to kill me if I had not been stronger than death. Take this, for instance:

"After I sold my first story for twenty-five dollars, I gave up my job and decided to live or die by my writing. The twenty-five dollars were soon used up. I was in the throes of my second story, and I was starving. I went to my sister. She had nine children. They never had enough to eat, but occasionally they let me have a bite from the little they had. The children were in the street when I arrived and my sister was next door at a neighbor's. My sister's house was always open. Poor people have no need to lock their homes. A pot of oatmeal was boiling on the stove. I seized the pot, rushed with it to the sink, added a little cold water to cool it and began wolfing it. That whole pot of oatmeal only whetted my hunger. There was a loaf of bread in the breadbox. Just as I started to break off a piece the children stormed in, and seeing me at their bread, tore it out of my hands. At this point my sister returned, saw the empty pot. Her shriek raised the roof of the flat.

"She threw up her hands, screaming, 'You're a wild animal——'

" 'I was so hungry——'

" '*You* were hungry? What about the children?'

" 'I don't live for myself——'

" 'For what do you live?'

" 'For my writing——'

" 'A writer she wants to be yet! A crazy wild animal, that's what you are. Stealing bread from starving children—that's worse than stealing pennies from a blind man's cup——'

" 'A mother has a right to steal to feed a hungry child. I have a right to steal to finish my story——'

" 'Who gives you the right? Your craziness gives you the right?'

" 'All right, then, I'm crazy. I'm a thief, a criminal. Call a policeman!' I shouted above the yells of the children. 'Say I've robbed. If it's a crime to want to give your thoughts to the world, then I'm a criminal. Send me to prison. I'll have something to eat till I finish my story. Some of the greatest books in the world were written in prison. Call the police. Let them lock me up.'

"I wish I could still justify the stealing of that oatmeal as I was able to fifteen years ago. But every step of my writing career was a brutal fight, like the stealing of that oatmeal from hungry children."

Even the waiters stopped removing plates and stood with the trays in their hands, listening openmouthed. One confession led to another.

"When I banked the money the movies paid me for *Hungry Hearts,* the elation of suddenly possessing a fortune was overshadowed by the voice of conscience: What is the difference between a potbellied boss who exploits the labor of helpless workers and an author who grows rich writing of the poor?"

When the applause came I felt as if I had walked out of darkness into light. Those young girls had struck the dead rock of frustration I had carried in my heart—and the living waters of life began to flow again.

There was something to being famous after all, I rejoiced. If I were a nobody, they would never have listened to me. They think I'm a success, and so my opinion is respected. I gave them something to think about.

But when they came crowding around me, murmuring, "It was so nice!" "So interesting!" "We'll never forget this thrilling evening!" the wonderful moment of exaltation when I felt at one with my audience began to fade.

Had it been only a fairy tale to them? Instead of showing them the barren road of my success, had I only sharpened their desire for it? In their shining eyes I saw the hunger for recognition at any price—their lust and mine for the glory of the limelight—the boom of the crowd that pursues a celebrity. Had my efforts to tell my story ended again in failure?

Another girl came up. "You're wonderful!" She shook my hand. "I only wish I had known you when you were poor and obscure."

I looked at her bright young face, surprised to see that it was already marked by anxiety.

"I'm working my way through college," she said. "I've been on my own since twelve."

She was so pretty! How could she have known poverty and look so gay, so decorative?

I turned to the other girls around me, my feeling of righteousness beginning to crumble. Just because they had never been starved enough to steal bread from hungry children, I had condemned them as callous and frivolous. The truth with which I wanted to shock them had been only the vanity of the injured showing off scars.

I had erected a wall of self-defense around me and shot arrows of envy at them. Immune to envy, immune to criticism, they swept across the wall and conquered me.

All at once I loved them. As I had made a bunch of confetti from my prepared speech, so I would have gladly made a bonfire of everything I had to feed the flame of their trusting youth.

PART THREE

CHAPTER I

THE SILENT YEARS

WITH THE leveling force of an earthquake, the stock crash of 1929 hit us all. Bankers, industrialists, ditch-diggers, and authors were tossed together into the same abyss.

Publishing houses were failing, magazines were folding up. I had stopped writing and royalties on my books had dwindled, then ceased. The closing of the Bank of the United States wiped out my savings; my investments were practically worthless.

It took some of the sting out of my misfortune to know that millions were suddenly as poor as I, that almost every one was affected by the hard times.

I moved from my sunny apartment on Fifth Avenue to a small flat on the lower West Side. Then to a darker, smaller flat in a shabbier house. I learned all over again to get along in a single housekeeping room until even that became too expensive. Then a rapid succession of cheaper, dingier rooms and cheaper, more crowded eating places.

The papers were full of projects to combat unemployment.

A committee to start recreation centers for the unemployed was headed by an author who had once been loud in praise of my work. I went to see her.

"What a pleasant surprise!" She greeted me with her ever-ready effusiveness. "And how are you?"

I could only stare at her in wonder at her ease, her high spirits. "You're as radiant as ever," I said. "I read in the papers of all you're doing for the unemployed." Then I plunged in and blurted, "I'm looking for a job——"

"You? You want a job?" The tone of her voice and the way she looked at me made me feel it was a crime to want a job. "What about your writing? I could stop eating easier than stop writing."

She was a voluptuous creature. Good food was in her face. She thrived on helping people.

"How could you stop?" she repeated.

"I started thinking and it silenced me."

Her big black eyes regarded me with a curious intentness.

"Have you written yourself out?" she asked blandly.

How could I explain what I was going through to this prolific author who wrote a story a month and a best seller a year and still had the energy to be a leading committee woman and a champion of the newest public-welfare projects?

I glanced about her chapel of achievement. The room with its stained-glass windows was like a medieval church. Saints looked down from the walls. Old parchments and books hand-lettered in fine vellum were placed with careful carelessness on one table. On another table there was a Florentine casket and from the partly opened lid tumbled colored Venetian beads.

"I wish I could live in a little hall room with a trunk under my bed," she murmured.

I smiled. "If you really had to live in a hall room with a trunk under your bed, you wouldn't find it so romantic."

"A writer can get along in a slum as well as in a palace."

A coldness came into her eyes. I could feel her curiosity giving way to fear. I had brought hall rooms too close to her. I looked at the red combs in her sleek black hair, red nail polish matching red lips. Her black satin dress accentuated the artificial pallor of her face.

"It's been nice seeing you," she said, taking me to the door. "I'll let you know if anything turns up."

I made other attempts to find work among those who had known me in my prosperous days. I met with the same frightened withdrawal. Friends retreated before my failing fortunes just as I had once run away from my own poor people.

My descent into obscurity had started before I had thought of looking for a job. Requests to lecture had declined. I never liked to lecture. I dreaded appearing on the platform. But when the offers no longer came, I missed them. No more fan letters, fewer letters from friends, fewer invitations for lunch and dinner. And then none at all.

Occasionally I ran into some of the celebrities with whom I used to dine at the Algonquin. At first I was naïve enough to greet them with the warmth I felt at sight of a familiar face. Only after I saw their embarrassment did I learn to avoid noticing them at all.

Perhaps it was my own fear, my own guilt for having failed, that frightened people away. But it seemed to me that everybody who had once sought me out now stoned me with silence. In a drugstore one night, a girl reporter who used to pursue me for interviews now could not see me, so busy was she having a prescription filled. Even casual acquaintances now gave me the marble stare and frozen heart.

Some one touched my shoulder on the street one afternoon.

"*Gevalt!* You look so skinny, so washed out!"

It was Sara Solomon, my shopmate of immigrant days. Her husband, a pants-presser, was now owner of a factory.

"We just moved to Riverside Drive. You have to ride up ten floors to get to me. From my windows you can see all New York." She regarded me from the height of her opulence. "And what's happened to you? Are you still so crazy for writing?"

"Crazier than ever!"

Sara shook her head. "Even when your picture was in all the papers, I knew you were *meshugeh* as a bedbug. I was always telling you that your head was on wheels, riding on air. With all your smartness—where did it get you?"

I smiled as I walked home. The last time I had heard from her was when she had written me in Hollywood, offering me the story of her life for the movies if she could get the same ten thousand dollars they had paid for mine.

As I sat in my room budgeting my last few dollars, some one knocked on the door. It was the roomer across the hall.

"They're talking about you on the radio!" she said excitedly. "Come and hear it!"

I walked into her room and heard a voice on the radio saying:

". . . and then for years this immigrant girl wrote and starved. One day she walked the city streets completely dejected. The thought of suicide entered her mind. She made her way back to her shabby room, dreading the landlady's demand for the overdue rent.

"As she entered, a slim, yellow envelope met her eyes. Who would be sending her a telegram? With trembling fingers she tore it open. The miracle had happened! A moving-picture agent wired that Hollywood was buying her book.

"The faith that had kept her at work through years of starvation was rewarded. She was sent to Hollywood.

"Today Anzia Yezierska knows fame and fortune. Yet without her faith, she might have remained an underprivileged immigrant—a poor, unknown factory worker. . . ."

The legend of my Cinderella success lived on while destitution stared me in the face.

I applied for a job at the Emergency Work Bureau. It took days of waiting in line before my turn came. The woman who interviewed applicants greeted me with a smile.

"Miss Yezierska! I've read your *Hungry Hearts*. We studied the book in social service courses."

"Oh, then you know me! Maybe you can help me."

"You want material for a new book?"

"I want a job."

She looked shocked. Her professional eye swept over me. "Are you absolutely destitute?"

"If I were, would I tell you?"

"Oh, in that case, would it be fair to rob a needy person of his job?"

"I didn't come to rob. I came to offer myself in any way you can use me."

She looked at me with weary impatience. "So many who come here want to be benefactors instead of beneficiaries. . . ."

"Aren't you yourself trying to be a benefactor?"

"But, my dear," she said, "that's different. I'm doing a job that needs to be done. I was among the first to start this bureau. The A.I.C.P. loaned me for this work."

"What is the A.I.C.P.?" I asked.

"That's the Association for Improving the Condition of the Poor. There are only about half a dozen of us experts in charge here. And we go back to the A.I.C.P. as soon as this emergency is over."

"I feel that I too could help in this work. I know the poor as no outsider could know them. I could answer telephones, interview people. . . ."

"All our work is taken care of by trained professionals, and we have a long list of unemployed social workers, teachers, and girls out of college waiting to be placed."

"Well, I could do publicity. Write the daily stories that . . ."

"That's in the hands of the John Price Jones Corporation."

"But they're just fund-raisers. Let them raise the money. Let me tell what happens to us who go begging for work——"

"The John Price Jones Corporation has its own staff."
She paused to take another appraising glance at my
clothes, then added, "Surely you must still be getting
royalties from your books. Our bureau is only for the
absolutely destitute."

I realized that to get a job I would have to avoid all
who had ever known me as a writer.

Sunday morning I went to the park with the Help
Wanted section tucked under my arm. I sat down, opened
the paper, but I found myself looking at the children.
Their eyes were wide-open, free from the fears and in-
trigues of the grownups around them. The mute guileless-
ness of those eyes made me aware of my sordid com-
promises to get on in the world.

I turned to the ads.

WANTED: RESPONSIBLE WOMAN CARE FOR CHILDREN
AFTER SCHOOL HOURS. PRIVATE ROOM IN BEAUTIFUL
HOME. SMALL SALARY. TELEPHONE MONDAY FOR AP-
POINTMENT.

I cut out the ad. I'll take that job, I decided. I had
always been drawn to children; now chance led me to
work I would love to do. Oh, for plain, honest work, simple tasks in silence, the peace of obscurity!

Early Monday morning I telephoned. A woman answered sleepily.

"What time is it?" she drawled. "I'm hardly awake
yet."

"It's seven. I know it's early, but I was so taken by
your ad!"

"Well, come over." She gave me an address on Washington Square.

I flew into the subway, released from weeks and months
of inaction. For the first time I knew what I wanted,
where I was going. I saw myself in the park, surrounded
by children, their eyes looking trustingly into mine.

The house surpassed my expectations. It was one of
the few red-brick homes left on Washington Square.

Peace, security flowed from the white colonial door with its polished brass. I looked up at the white curtained windows, visualizing the room that would be mine: a room facing the sunny quiet of green trees. The morning sun gilded the autumn colors of the ivy against the red brick, wrapping the house in an aura of timelessness. "Small salary . . ." I would work without pay, just to be with children in such a beautiful house.

A butler showed me into the reception room. Home, this feels like a real home, I thought, looking around. Through an arched door I saw a bronze vase with yellow roses on a piano. There would be music here.

"Mrs. Ward will be down shortly," the butler said.

Two blond-haired little girls looked in shyly. I beckoned to them. "Come and talk to me."

"Are you going to be our nurse?" the older girl asked, her eyes looking into mine.

The other touched my hand and thrust her picture book at me. "Take off your hat and stay. . . ."

"You like stories? I'll tell you a story from these pictures. I'm a storyteller."

In a moment, their shyness gone, they drew close to me. I opened the book. "Once upon a time . . ."

Mrs. Ward, tall and straight, walked in. Her brisk smile appraised the scene. "Your voice sounded so young over the phone. How old are you?"

"I'm not as old as I look." I tried to smile, but under her scrutiny I felt a fool.

"I'm afraid the work will be too strenuous for you."

"Oh, Mother!" the little one begged, and reached for my hand. "Let her stay! Please, Mummy."

"Judith, we have something to talk about. You and Evelyn go upstairs."

After they had gone, Mrs. Ward turned to me. "You won't do. The children have to have their clothes changed twice a day. Their wash requires a husky person."

"I'm stronger than I look."

"And they're so wild in their play. . . ."

"I love children. Even their wildness I love."

"Well, give me your name and telephone number and I'll let you know."

"There's no telephone where I live. Should I call you?"

She frowned at my persistence. "Where's the last place you've worked?"

"I . . . I haven't worked for any one for years. That is . . . you see . . . I was a writer. . . ."

"A writer?" Suspicion tightened her lips.

"I'm not writing any more," I explained. "I can apply the same intelligence to the care of children as I once did to writing."

"I need some one young and strong who can do the children's wash and keep them clean." She stood up, dismissal in her eyes. "I need a nursemaid, not a writer."

CHAPTER II

THE NEW POOR

THE MATTER-OF-FACT way in which Mrs. Ward had looked me over and dismissed me as unfit to be a nurse-maid was a slap in the face that jolted me out of my egoism, my aloofness from life. The vanity of dreaming that I could find peace in obscurity while the country rocked with the depression! This was no time for peace. Destitute millions of unemployed roamed the highways, hungry, homeless. I was one of them.

Every day I saw more men and women used to enjoying middle-class security in the waiting lines of unemployed. Teachers begged for jobs in department stores. Architects and onetime landlords raked leaves and picked trash in parks. The once industrious white-collar class—stenographers, librarians, accountants—were busy making themselves eligible for the dole. People who had put their trust in gilt-edged bonds now met the old poor in bread lines, in soup kitchens, in the waiting rooms of emergency-relief stations.

Everywhere, on almost every block I passed, I saw evictions. Decent, hard-working people were tossed into the scrapheap. Their jobs, their places in life, all their old values were swept away. They sat in the streets hunched over their last possessions.

The old poor had nothing to lose in the failing banks and the crashing market. They had always known want. Hardened to worry, immune to fear, they good-naturedly made room for the new poor, their onetime betters. There was always room at the bottom.

It was the new poor who suffered the terrors of the hard times. My landlady lost her penny-hoarded savings and could not pay rent. Faced with the threat of eviction, we huddled together and shared our little as we had never shared our plenty. The less we had, the friendlier we grew, the gayer our laughter. Misery had found company.

Since jobs were not to be had, our chief pastime was going to Union Square, the meeting place of the unemployed. On the benches were men and women of every class. Old men in rags, vagrants from the Bowery, young radicals ready to change the world, jobless school teachers and shoe clerks, lonely old women and girl graduates, uprooted victims of the depression.

I got to know the homeless ones who spent their days on benches and slept at night in hallways and on the stone floors of subway stations.

One man with a shock of wonderful white hair and a grim, unshaven face seemed to me the Everyman of the homeless. His eyes were glazed in silence—a silence beyond despair.

One morning I sat down beside him, offering him a cigarette. He took it without a smile, without a word. Defeat had set his face into lines of irreparable sadness.

"I happen to have a man's sweater at home," I said. "It's about your size. I'll bring it tomorrow."

His jaw snapped. "I don't need it!"

"You know you need it——"

"In the gutter you need nothing."

"You're too intelligent to remain in the gutter."

He looked at me for a moment, and then his gaze drifted far out. "Have you ever been in the Bowery? There you'll see many others like me."

"But you're not like those others. You're a man who thinks."

He stood up in his rags. "I hate pity. I can't stand any one trying to be kind."

And he walked away, tall and straight, with the dignity of a man immune to adversity.

There were young girls at Union Square, girls who had come to the city in search of work and were now penniless. Their stories were the same: they had lost their jobs and they could not go back to their upstate homes and become burdens to their families. There were older men and women, recruits of the new poor, daily becoming thinner, grayer, and shabbier. Hunger and homelessness had leveled them all and dulled their eyes with the same look of defeat. And then one day some one handed us leaflets:

UNEMPLOYED, UNITE! FIGHT FOR JOBS!
FIGHT TOGETHER!

As I read, I heard drums. Men and women were assembling. They carried placards:

WE WANT JOBS—JOBS—NOT CHARITY!
WE ARE WORKERS—NOT PAUPERS!
WE WANT WORK!

A voice in the crowd started singing:

"Arise, ye prisoners of starvation,
Arise, ye wretched of the earth.
For justice thunders condemnation.
A better world's in birth. . . ."

The band struck up and the marchers joined in the song. Voices in ever-increasing volume took up the chant. It was a stirring spectacle. A mad parade of shouting men and women, but their cry was charged with exaltation. "Jobs! Jobs! Put the bankers on relief! We want work!"

A bony old woman with gray disheveled hair thrust a placard into my hand. All the poor I had ever known looked at me out of the toothless mouth of her ravaged face.

"Come! March with us!" she coaxed, clapping me on the shoulder. "Join our cry for work!"

Like one in a trance, bewitched by the familiarity of the face, I fell into step. All that I had fled all my days caught up with me. In spite of the hysteria and madness of the parade, the warming earthiness of the people was so intoxicating that I no longer feared to be poor. I no longer feared fear.

Other onlookers like myself were drawn in by the marchers, caught up by the gospel—work. The crowd kept growing. The procession swelled to include all the unemployed of the street. And I was marching and shouting and singing with the others!

~~~~~~

CHAPTER III

RELIEF

A NEW life opened to me with my new-found young friends, the jobless writers and painters. Night after night, I joined their meetings at Stewart's Cafeteria. For a five-cent cup of coffee we could sit for hours, discussing the one topic of conversation among hungry people everywhere—jobs.

They were in the midst of planning another hunger march to Washington when Harold Gordon, the organizer of the Unemployed Artists' Union, came in waving the evening edition of the morning tabloid.

"We did it! It's come! It's here!"

He spread the newspaper out on the table and every one followed the words as he read the headlines:

PRESIDENT SECURES FOUR BILLION DOLLARS TO CREATE EMPLOYMENT

SPECIAL PROJECTS FOR ACTORS, PAINTERS, MUSICIANS, WRITERS

These were the people who had worked for it. The old-timers had been planning this for months, years. Petitions, demonstrations, picket lines, mass delegations, leaflets to unemployed to join the fight for jobs. At last it had come. We read it over and over again.

FOUR BILLION DOLLARS FOR JOBS . . .

One after another picked up the newspaper, disbelieving. Perhaps because they had fought so hard for it they were stunned. It was too good to be true. And when they were finally convinced that their dream was about to be realized, the discussion became a joyous shouting celebration.

A new world was being born. A world where artists were no longer outcasts, hangers-on of the rich, but backed by the government, encouraged to produce their best work.

The President said so.

People who no longer hoped or believed in anything but the end of the world began to hope and believe again.

In the weeks that followed, radios boomed with it. Everywhere—at grocers, cigar stores, lunch counters, in the streets—people were discussing the President's plan to end unemployment. Every day we read announcements in the newspapers of the prominent men and women appointed by the President to direct the various departments of W.P.A.

One morning as I was in the kitchen of my rooming house fixing breakfast, the radio broadcast a special news item about W.P.A.: a headquarters had just been set up for the new Writers' Project. I hurried to the address, eager to work. Ever since I had marched with the unemployed I was full of ideas for stories. All I needed to begin writing again was the security of a W.P.A. wage to get my typewriter out of the pawnshop.

A drab office building of narrow windows and faded stone housed the Writers' Project. Newly painted government signs stood out against the scarred, dirty walls.

In the lobby I joined the crowd heading toward the elevator. A uniformed guard stopped us.

"Freight elevator!" he barked.

"What's wrong with the passenger elevator in the front?" some one asked.

"That's for officials only."

As we scrambled through the long dark hall to the back

of the building, I recalled the Free Vacation House of immigrant days. We for whom the house had been donated were consigned to the back part. The front of the house was reserved for the board of directors meetings. We charity vacationists sat on long wooden benches in the back yard, furtively spying on the committee ladies in the front parlor, planning our food and directing our destinies.

The freight elevator was in use moving office equipment. We lined up behind a rope, waiting to get on. In the noisy confusion of loading and unloading, more people kept coming, joining the crowd behind the rope. Some shabby, well-pressed gentility held aloof, edging closer to their own kind. The rest of us were intent only on getting into the elevator.

At last the guard raised the rope. With the crowd, I was pushed into the elevator and dumped on the twelfth floor. White placards above rows of desks indicated the various departments.

I walked up to the guard at the first desk.

"I've come to work on the Writers' Project——"

"What's your relief number?"

"I don't want relief. I want work as a writer."

"You have to be on relief to get on W.P.A.," he stated.

"Isn't there a ten per cent quota who do not have to go through relief?"

"Those are the big names. They have already been chosen," he said and turned to the next applicant.

I walked away, remembering stories I had heard of what people had to go through at the relief mill. Then I thought of Harold Gordon. He had been among the first to get on W.P.A.

I went to his loft on West Third Street under the shadow of the El. Seated about his cluttered studio, young people were drinking and laughing.

"Hi, Yezierska!" Gordon hailed me. "Have a beer and catch up with us. We're celebrating payday."

"Did all of you have to go through relief?" I asked.

"What in hell did you expect? Utopia?" Gordon demanded. "They have to handle crowds of people. And so they resort to charity methods of administration."

"I still don't see why we have to become paupers to get work."

A dark, solemn-faced young girl turned on me. "Why do you make such a fuss? We all had to go through it. Look at me. I'm supposed to be an art teacher. I have a diploma from Hunter. But the schools aren't appointing any new teachers, and on the Art Project a diploma is nothing. You've got to be a goddamn charity case."

She had had to swear to the relief authorities that her mother was dead, that she had no home, no means of support.

"Sure I got a mother." The girl gave a bitter imitation of a laugh. "Mother keeps roomers, but most of them are out of work. My mother's close to the bread line, but that would make no difference to them."

As long as she had a home, she explained, it made her ineligible for work on the Art Project. She was forced to build up a careful structure of lies to prove that she was living with another girl: letters from friends to that address, testimony from others that she was destitute.

"At least you're *working* for your money—not rotting away," an oldish woman consoled.

"Listen! Going on relief is just like passing an examination," a red-lipped girl advised. "There's nothing to it. Just remember the rules: Two years' residence in the city. No relatives. No friends. No insurance. No money. No nothing—you've got to be starving to death."

A tall, gaunt man with an enormous black mustache added helpfully, "You've got to be careful about the two years' residence. Now, I've been in the city only a month, but I proved the required two years' residence okay. I had a friend say that I lived in her house. She gave me some of her mail and I rubbed out her name with ink eradicator and put my own name on it."

"I couldn't do that," I protested.

"It's being done by the best people," Gordon assured me.

I was so horrified that they stopped their laughter.

"What's the good of a job if you have to sell your soul for it?"

"For Christ's sake! Don't be so tragic! You need a job, don't you? To hell with pride. The relief mill has to put the stamp of a legalized pauper on your forehead. Shut your eyes and go through with it. It's like having a tooth pulled."

Next morning I stood in line again, waiting for the doors of Home Relief to open. Endless hours we stood on the sidewalk where passers-by could stare at us creeping one step at a time—only to meet at the door the uniform with the brass badge: "That's all for this morning. Come back this afternoon."

Afternoon. More waiting in line. When we got inside, the waiting began once again. Misery huddled on benches; bent heads, furtive eyes watched the investigators at their desks. The air was a hot, greasy fog. If they would only open the windows— But so drained from waiting were we all, no one had the courage to approach the guard.

"How long? God! How long?" some one whispered.

A bearded youth with bloodshot eyes took up the whisper. "Christ! I'm hungry! My head is splitting!"

"Why don't you try Christian Science?" another mocked.

"Thanks! I'd rather have ham and eggs."

Next to them sat an old woman locked in silence. All at once the air was torn by her hysterical shriek. "How much longer you make me wait? You bastards!"

I jumped up to aid the woman.

"Number thirty-nine!" My relief number was called. At the voice of authority, instead of going to the woman, I automatically walked to the desk.

The investigator looked me over as I sat down.

Then the questioning began. "Name? . . . Address? . . . Name of your father? . . . Have you any brothers?

Sisters? Husband? Children? . . . Where were you born?
Have you any money saved? How much rent do you pay?
Can any member of your family, relative, or friend support you? Have you a piano, a radio, automobile . . .
anything you could turn into money? Do you have any
insurance that could be cashed?"

He scribbled my answers on a printed form. "How did
you live until now? You had a hundred dollars three
months ago? What did you do with it? How long have
you lived in New York? Before that? And before that?
Have you proof of these statements?"

"You'll have to take my word for it."

"Where would we be if we took every one's word? All
right, that's all. Go home and wait till your case is in-
vestigated."

So the waiting began again. Each knock, each ring of
the bell put me in a cold sweat of excitement. I could not
read. I could not see friends. I could only wait.

At last the investigator brought me a food check with
a number on a ticket. I had successfully passed the relief
test. Hooray! I was a pauper!

I rushed to the Writers' Project. I thrust my ticket
into the hands of the application clerk. "I have it! I have
it! I have my number. Now I'm eligible for work!"

The man smiled at my elation. "Very well. I'll take this
up with our personnel man."

"When do I start to work?"

"I'll get in touch with you."

"I'm ready. I have my ticket. Oh, God, how long I've
waited!"

"Every one has to wait."

A day passed. Another, and another. And still I waited.
At every delivery I hurried to the mailbox. I questioned
the janitor. No use. There was nothing for me.

At last I got the relief clerk on the telephone. "You
said you would get in touch with me."

"You'll have to wait your turn. You're on our list."

Wait again? Weeks had already passed, waiting. Nothing but waiting. Waiting, tortured by the hope of work . . .

I picked up the food check and stared at the printed name—my name—and over it the words "HOME RELIEF BUREAU." And then a number. A number for a dole. The hope of work ended in a food check.

I tore the card to pieces, tossed them into the wastebasket.

I stormed out of the house. I did not know where I was going or what I would do. But I would starve rather than submit to the demoralization of relief any longer.

The air of the street cooled the turmoil within me. Suddenly, everything I had been through became clear. I had to write it. Write it to President Roosevelt himself. Is this "upholding the hands of the forgotten man"? Grinding him through a relief mill more deadly than the old-time charities? Holding out hope of work to the unemployed—only to madden them with hopeless waiting?

It was evening when I returned. Automatically, I stopped at the little table in the hall where the mail was spread. There was a letter from the Works Progress Administration. I tore open the envelope and read:

You have been appointed to the Writers' Project. $23.86 per week.

The ticket! I ran upstairs. I looked into the wastebasket. Thank God! I sat down on the floor and fitted the torn pieces carefully together again.

CHAPTER IV

WORKING FOR THE GOVERNMENT

THE AMAZING resilience of people! How they cling to life, even on the edge of an abyss!

In the smoky half-light of the waiting room, faces rushed to me in a whirl of color and sound. I had seen these people at the relief station, waiting for the investigating machine to legalize them as paupers. Now they had work cards in their hands. Their waiting was no longer the hopeless stupor of applicants for mass relief; they were employees of the government. They had risen from the scrap heap of the unemployed, from the loneliness of the unwanted, dreaming of regeneration, together. The new job look lighted the most ravaged faces.

"Thank God for the depression!" a tall, gaunt man spouted. "The depression fathered W.P.A.!" His tattered coat hung loose on his shrunken body. A safety pin fastened the frayed collar of his shirt. Unaware of his rags, his ghastly appearance, he fixed his eyes on me. "Roosevelt will go down to posterity as the savior of art in America."

"The savior of art!" I laughed. "At the bargain price of $23.86 per artist."

He ignored the jibe and pointed to the brief case under his arm. "My worries for a living are over. Now I can devote myself to my real work, *The Life of Spinoza*." He hugged his brief case as if it were a living thing. "Here are all my notes—every word written in blood."

A cough interrupted the flow of his words and heightened the flush of his cheeks. He regained his breath and went on. "Great books that had no chance before will see the light of the day. The Congressional Library will become the Bodleian of the world."

A young Negro stood listening with the calm smile of a young Buddha. His well-modeled head on straight-built shoulders stood out among the white-faced men drained by defeat.

"Young man, you don't agree, do you?"

He went on smiling.

"Your face is young, but you have an old head on your shoulders," I said.

He laughed softly. "Born old, I guess."

I glanced at the card in his hand and read the name Richard Wright. Struck by the serenity of this youth, I asked, "What kind of writing do you do?"

"Unpublished writing." His laughter was a window flung open in the smoke-filled room. "This is the biggest break I ever had. For the first time the government is giving us bread and meat."

"Isn't it wonderful that all of us writers with so many different stories should all be the concern of the government?"

"Don't glorify a tent for a night—a soup kitchen in time of famine," said Richard Wright.

"But we mustn't let it be a soup kitchen, a tent for a night," the ragged old man protested. "W.P.A. must be made a permanent institution, a new National Academy of Arts." A lock of hair, brushed to cover the bald spot, stood up stubbornly as he thumped with his cane to accentuate his words. "This is the richest country in the world. There's money for the Army, the Navy, for wars. Why not for life? For art and the creators of art?"

He took out a folder of clippings from an envelope. With gentle fingers, he touched his picture at the head of a Jewish news column, tattered and yellowed with age, but carefully reinforced with glue strips.

"Read." He pushed the yellowed clippings into my lap. The picture was that of a dreaming boy of twenty. I read phrases from the clipping: "Brilliant essayist . . . scholarly thinker . . . we predict a great future for Jeremiah Kintzler . . ."

"Jeremiah Kintzler is my name." Deep wrinkles about his mouth joined those of his eyes as he smiled at his picture, catching its young reflection in his old face.

"What a beautiful name!" I said.

"I once occupied the editorial chair of a Hebrew monthly written by the Warsaw Yeshivah." His voice mounted into a rhapsodic chant. "I've compiled a history of talmudic literature and I'm the author of *Baal Sham Tov,* a study of one of the greatest Hebrew mystics of the last four hundred years. Besides, I have my *Life of Spinoza* almost finished."

He put the folder of clippings back into his brief case.

The intensity that frustration had etched on his face was as familiar to me as the sight and smells of the ghetto streets that I loved and hated.

"All your manuscripts you carry with you?" I asked, seeing how tenderly he held his bulging brief case.

"Should I leave them in my room?" He was shocked. "Suppose a fire breaks out?"

I looked from the furrowed forehead and dream-ridden eyes of the old Jew to the smooth-faced young Negro. One reminded me of so much that I knew and wanted to forget; the other opened a new, unknown world. I wondered whether it was harder to be born a Jew in a Christian world than a Negro—a black skin in a white world.

My name was called and I jumped up.

"We must meet again," Jeremiah Kintzler said. "I want to show you——"

"Let's all meet again after our assignments," I said, and followed the guard into the office.

John Barnes, the director, drew up a chair for me at his desk. He was a tall, very thin man with a long face and a sad mouth. His well-tailored clothes, and some-

thing scholarly in his manner, at first reminded me of
the men I had met in the days when I went to literary
teas.

"Anzia Yezierska." He shook hands. I smelled the
liquor on his breath and saw the unguarded gleam of his
eyes. "What brings you here?"

"The same thing that has brought thousands of others
to W.P.A."

A pause. A long silence.

"You know, I used to review your books in the old
days," he said.

"That immigrant stuff was so long ago, in a past existence. When I stopped turning it out, I saw my own
funeral procession go by."

He smiled so understandingly that I stopped talking.
His eyes seemed to see at a glance all I had been through,
and they made anything I might say in defense of myself superfluous. How amazing, I thought, that after all
the deaths I had died I could still be so alive to a little
bit of friendliness, and I heard myself talk again.

"What a story Dostoevski could write of the poor people here!"

"Dostoevski's dead," he said, offering me a cigarette.
"You write it."

I waved the cigarette aside. "There's a man out there
in the waiting room," I said. "A skeleton in rags with a
brief case. He looks like the Ancient Mariner with the
dead albatross on his neck. If any one here knew enough
to write his story, he'd know what God and man is."

Barnes looked at me in silence. With fumbling fingers,
he relit his cigarette. After a pause he said, "Why don't
you write it, or better still, have you thought of writing
your own story?"

The telephone rang. Barnes picked up the receiver, and
after a pause snorted, "Well, Somervell! What do you
want me to do? Stand over them and watch them do
their work? I'm not a timekeeper."

He raised his voice to a querulous shout. "Boondoggling—hell! What can you expect of people who haven't worked so long they've forgotten how? Remember, they were hired because they were on relief. I can't park on their tails every minute."

He slammed down the receiver. "Christ! I give up! An army man in charge of the Writers' Project! But of course it's not a Writers' Project—it's a landmark in nonsense. All the misfits and maniacs on relief have been dumped here."

His eyes shone with the brilliance of exhaustion, lit up with the aid of drink.

"Can you imagine what it is to keep six hundred bums busy with the pretense of writing?"

Liquor was getting him to the point of tears. "The phoniness, the stupidity that I have to put up with," he wailed. "I was a poet. Now I'm a glorified office boy."

He checked himself. "I'm an awful lush. But you've got an idea. See what you can make out of it. Even an army man wouldn't mind having a good autobiography come out of W.P.A.!"

As I walked out, the old man laid a bony hand on my arm and reminded me that I had said that we must meet again. He wanted to celebrate working for the government by treating me to a cup of coffee.

"*Nu?* Can you refuse me?" he pleaded.

"How can I refuse you?"

Over our coffee he confided to me why Spinoza was the great passion of his life.

"I know Spinoza better than I know myself. When I wake up in the middle of the night, I sometimes feel that *I'm* Spinoza!"

̂̂

CHAPTER V

THE NEW SOCIETY
OF ARTS AND LETTERS

ON THE first payday everybody went to Tony's Bar to cash his check. I followed, swept along by the wild elation. While the bartender was on the way to the bank we sat around the bar nibbling free pretzels. When the money arrived we treated one another to beer with the magnanimity of new millionaires. Then we crowded into the smoke-filled banquet hall at the rear of the bar, ordered a feast—a thirty-five-cent table-d'hôte dinner— and tossed nickel tips to the waiter. We were as hilarious as slum children around a Christmas tree. Pockets jingled with money. Men who hadn't had a job in years fondled five- and ten-dollar bills with the tenderness of farmers rejoicing over new crops of grain.

"Friends! Quiet, please!" Barnes stood up, and with a wave of his hand, brought silence. "I'd like to say a few words. But for heaven's sake, don't consider me a 'boss.' I've been unemployed just like the rest of you. We've all been kicked around. Suddenly we're handed an opportunity to really become human beings again. We have to live up to the responsibility of this trust. Who knows, among us even now may be a new Gorky, a new Dostoevski."

One after another rose to give his testimonial of faith.

"Folks!" Richard Wright said jubilantly. "Where I come from, they're all singing:

161

"Roosevelt! You're my man!
When the time come
I ain't got a cent,
You buy my groceries
And pay my rent.
Mr. Roosevelt, you're my man!

"But now we've been given more than a bellyful of
grub. The President has given us Negroes a chance at
last, and I tell you I mean to make the most of it. I've
had all kinds of jobs. I've shined shoes, washed dishes,
I've been a Pullman porter, I've scrubbed floors, cleaned
toilets. Those are nigger jobs. Some folks think that's all
we're fit for—art is only for white folks. This is the greatest day of my life. I'm just rarin' to go. . . ."

I turned to Barnes as Wright sat down. "We are lucky
to have a man like you for our director. You're a poet,
not a boss, and that's what we need. I feel like a bit of
withered moss that has been suddenly put into water,
growing green again. Give people a ray of hope and they
rise out of their ashes and begin to dream and live again."

Bill Adams, a dark sallow-faced youth with sad old
eyes, burst into mirthless laughter. "To hear you people
talk, one would think the millennium had come. A rotten
tree can only bear rotten fruit. All they're after is to
prime their voting machine to keep their busted capi-
talistic system going. . . ."

"Lay off, stinker!"

"Dry up!"

Voices of disapproval were heard from every corner of
the room; even the Marxists of the group were too joyous at that moment to tolerate their gloomy ideologist.
Bill Adams went on, unheeding.

"Mass bribery, that's what W.P.A. is. Government
blackmail. We'd fight, we'd stage riots and revolutions
if they didn't hush us up. We're all taking hush money.
But if we were smart, we'd take the money and keep
hollering."

He flicked the ash from his cigarette. "The Mellons and

the Morgans and the holy crusaders of the Liberty League must laugh when they think how cheaply they silenced the voice of an entire class and averted a revolution with a few billions of the people's money."

A diabolical grin distorted his face. "They're going to kill us off soon enough in the next war. This sop to hunger, the W.P.A., is our prewar bonus. Folks, that's a hot one! Instead of calling it Works Progress Administration, we ought to call it Victims for Future Wars!"

He was shouted down at last. Jeremiah Kintzler stood up. He put down his cane and his brief case, drew out his identification card and waved it in the air.

"There are cynics who say that there are black spots in the shining sun. Those cynics will tell you that this ticket is only an admission number to the bread line, only hush money to avert a revolution. But I tell you this is a passport to a new world. A membership ticket to our new Society of Arts and Letters. A society where each human being will have bread for the body, work for the soul."

Carefully he replaced the relief ticket in his breast pocket, lifted his brief case, the guileless look of a child in his eyes.

"Here is the labor of fifty years! For fifty years I hoped and dreamed and prayed over every word written here. I've knocked at the door of every publisher. Did I ask money? Did I want something from them? No! I only wanted to give them my life." He paused, choked with emotion. "Fifty years of hopes and dreams and prayers, and they rejected me. They laughed at me. They treated me like a common beggar. Now you wonder why I love that man Roosevelt? He vindicated me and my *Life of Spinoza*. The President has commanded me to arise and shine, for a light has come!"

Richard Wright leaped to his feet, took up the refrain. "Rise and shine! That was one of the great songs that led my people out of slavery." He began to sway and chant. "Rise and shine! Give God the glory, glory!"

Laughing voices took up the refrain. The walls re-

sounded with clapping hands and stamping feet in Holy
Roller syncopation.

> "Rise and shine!
> Give God the glory, glory!
> Rise and shine!"

Every day new events fired our enthusiasm. A week
later, there was a crowd at the bulletin board reading the
announcement of lectures to be held at the Writers'
Union: Theodore Dreiser on the novel, Stephen Vincent
Benét on poetry, and Sherwood Anderson on the short
story.

"How is this for a literary workshop?" Paul Yellin addressed the crowd. "Those famous authors are coming
down to talk to you man to man—writers to writers. We're
bringing you the master-craftsmen of America. You've
got the blocks, and those big guys are going·to show you
how to put your blocks together."

He paused to look at their shining faces.

"And now we've got some business to attend to," he
went on. "We still have to fight to keep our jobs. That
takes dough, fellers. We need money for leaflets, for
picket signs, for delegations to Washington. I expect
every one of you to cough up your two bits today. Free
riders and chiselers will see their names on the bulletin
board."

Jeremiah Kintzler put down his brief case and waved
his cane. "I'm an artist. I'm not interested in propa-
ganda. Leaflets, picket signs—what do they mean to a
writer? But if the union is going in for culture, for art,
here's my quarter. Here are two quarters." With solemn
dignity he walked to the table and put down his two
quarters. "You want more yet? So I won't have breakfast tomorrow. But I'm the first to support the artist's
life."

"Okay, brother, okay." Yellin's smile was reflected in
all their faces. "We're going in for culture with a cap-
ital C."

CHAPTER VI

FELLOWSHIP OF NECESSITY

EACH MORNING I walked to the Project as light-hearted as if I were going to a party. The huge, barracks-like Writers' Hall roared with the laughter and greetings of hundreds of voices. As we signed in, we stopped to smoke, make dates for lunch and exchange gossip. Our grapevine buzzed with budding love affairs, tales of salary raises, whispers of favoritism, the political maneuvers of the big shots, and the way Barnes told off Somervell over the phone. There was a hectic camaraderie among us, although we were as ill-assorted as a crowd on a subway express—spinster poetesses, pulp specialists, youngsters with school-magazine experience, veteran newspaper men, art-for-art's-sake literati, and the clerks and typists who worked with us—people of all ages, all nationalities, all degrees of education, tossed together in a strange fellowship of necessity.

There was old Jeremiah Kintzler, urging everybody to write to the President to abolish the Army and Navy and set up a "permanent Society of Arts and Letters of America," and young Richard Wright, as yet unpublished and unknown, but always the center of the serious aspirants to literature.

There was also Edwin Peck, a former professor of English, an authority on *Beowulf* and Chaucer, who stood aloof from the social caldron. His eyes were sunk so deep in their sockets that you could see no color, no light in them. The reverses that drew others together separated him and carved on his gray face the loneliness of his pride.

Another figure of proud isolation was Priscilla Howard, a thin, white-haired New England spinster. Each day when she stood in line to sign in with the loud, pushing mob, she felt an alien in her own country. Her shoulders shrank in fastidious protest at this horde of foreigners who neither knew nor cared that her ancestors had landed in 1620. She always wore earrings, a brooch and a ring of flowered mosaic, heirlooms of her English ancestors, and her fingers, with their swollen knuckles, would hold onto her brooch in fierce protectiveness. She was born a Howard, and she would always bear herself like a Howard.

It was hard for Miss Howard to talk to any of us, and after a few rebuffs we left her alone. But Pat Ryan and Paul Yellin, the gregarious leaders of the Writers' Union, had a mission. Every one on the Project was to them a brother- or a sister-worker to be won over to the union.

That this Irishman and Jew should consider themselves relatives of hers and should want her to join their union so outraged Miss Howard that she told them who she was and why she would have nothing to do with them. But automatically she was handed the same literature we all got, union leaflets, political tracts, and even *Red Pen,* which she conspicuously tore up and threw into the wastebasket. Ryan and Yellin ignored this minor rebellion.

No two men on the Project were more unlike in background and personality than our union leaders. Blond Pat Ryan had been a world traveler and lecturer; Paul Yellin was a dark young Jew from the gutters of the ghetto, who had worked without pay on a Left Wing magazine. Ryan's big-boned athletic body exuded the ease of a man who enjoyed every moment of life. Yellin was short, stocky, grim-faced, with a stubborn intensity born of poverty. But the two had one thing in common—their passion for the union. No doubts, no confusion, no introspective questioning wasted them. They had nothing but the relief tickets that entitled them to their jobs on W.P.A., but they carried themselves with an assurance that millionaires might envy. They had nothing, and because they had nothing, they believed themselves destined by historic forces to change the world.

Yellin was the only supervisor who still wore his old work clothes, the only untamed peasant among the white-collared gentility who sat on swivel chairs behind desks marked "Supervisor." The desks were new. The men at their new jobs wore brand-new suits; you could almost see the price tags dangling from their crisp new ties. But Yellin wasn't in their class. Every cent saved from bare necessities and every free moment went to the union.

Yellin and Ryan were brave men, for not even Finley, the guard, could intimidate them. At first they tried to win him over to a realization that he was a worker and should favor the workers. But Finley, swaggering in his new uniform with brass buttons, was born to keep discipline for the bosses. He loved to bellow, "Keep in line there! Where's your card? No card? Then stay out!" He snorted with satisfaction whenever he had a chance to vent his authority and push people back into place.

The only person he never pushed around was red-haired Jean Williams. Finley melted when she smiled at him. Jean was young and beautiful and as free as thistle-down from the cares that weighed on others. She wore a soft black jersey that showed every curve of her body —she had nothing to hide. Men's eyes followed her, and she accepted their admiration as naturally as their free dinners. She was so friendly she could even make women forget their jealousy.

The first time I saw her was at Tony's, where we cashed our checks. She was sitting at the bar as we came in, and she pushed aside an empty glass, opened her compact and outlined her mouth with lipstick. Bill Adams stared in fascination.

"Are you on the Project?" he asked. "I haven't seen you before."

She looked at him with newly reddened lips. "I wish I were." Her husky voice had a vibrant eagerness. "You writers are having such a swell time. You get paid every week. I never know where my dinner's coming from."

He ordered her a drink. "Why don't you get on too?"

"For one thing, I'm not a writer." She laughed. "I'm an artist's model. But I've always wanted to write——"

"The story of your life?"

"How did you guess?"

"It's in your eyes." He patted her knee. "I'll make a writer of you. Just get on relief."

She widened her eyes at him. "Wouldn't that be an awful thing to go through? I don't want any of those reliefers prying into my affairs."

"But it's very simple. I know an investigator who'll do anything for you, if you're nice to him."

Jean threw back her head and laughed. "Lead me to him."

"Baby! You stick with me. I'll do the writing for you, too."

Arm in arm, they walked out. One of the men at the bar set down his glass and shook his head in mock bitterness. "Why can't a man sleep his way into a job like those luscious babes?"

"Brother," a woman writer retorted, "bitching from bed to bed is specialized work."

Two weeks later, with a relief card in her hand, Jean was on her way to the personnel head of the Project. She quickly got to know everybody.

I was lucky to be on the Creative Project. Those who worked on the *Guide* had to sign in each morning at nine, get their assignments from their editors, and sign out at four. I did my writing at home and had to report once a week to Barnes.

After he had read a rough draft of my day-to-day story

of W.P.A., he said. "You're still too close to it to get to the meaning that will come later on. Perhaps you're trying to say too many things at the same time."

"Well, there's so much to write. I'm so anxious to show something for my time."

"Don't be too anxious," Barnes said. "Writing that amounts to anything takes a lot of time. The Creative Project was meant to give writers a chance to work in peace and confidence."

He picked up a publicity release. "This is what I have to submit to the Colonel. 'The total production of six hundred writers for the past week was 1,200,000 words, an average of two thousand words per writer.'" He flung the page aside. "These millions of words will never see the light of day. In the end we'll have to hire professional journalists to do the guidebooks."

I was not the only one who found a friend in Barnes. He drew to himself all the odd ones of the Project, among them Jeremiah Kintzler.

But Jeremiah refused to submit any part of his *Life of Spinoza* for approval. "Creative work cannot be judged until it is finished," he said, and asked me to go with him when he protested to Barnes.

"It's true that no one is fit to judge creative work until it's done," Barnes conceded. "But in order to get our subsidy, we must send a record of each writer's work to Washington."

Jeremiah's hand tightened on his brief case. "I cannot violate my integrity as an artist and show work before it is perfect."

Barnes glanced at me, then turned back to Jeremiah. After a silence he said, "You're the best judge of what you can do. Go on with your *Life of Spinoza* in your own way, and good luck to you."

Jeremiah grasped his hand, shook it warmly. "Long life on you! It takes an artist to respect the integrity of another artist." He went out beaming and waving his cane.

As the door closed, Barnes turned to me. "The vanity that burns in that skeleton of a man! No doubt he sleeps with his brief case for a pillow. His old head can find no rest apart from his dreams."

"It takes so little to make him happy," I said. "Only a chance to talk about his work."

"I like the old bum," Barnes said. "I wish some one would clean him up."

"But he'd fight God and the angels to defend the right to his dirt."

Barnes lit a cigarette, smoked in silence a few minutes, then said, "Jeremiah's the symbol of all of us here—deformities struggling to be gods."

Even the leaders of the union thought Barnes a good fellow. Once a week when the union delegation had their meeting with Barnes in his office to present their grievances and new demands, it was done with great formality.

Pat Ryan, the president of the union, and Paul Yellin, the executive secretary, maintained that to keep what we had, we had to stay on the offensive and persistently make demands for better working conditions and more pay.

And then one day the weekly union delegation meeting with Barnes coincided with one of his daytime binges. He was bleary-eyed and met the delegation with a frown. Pat Ryan ignored Barnes's mood and proceeded with the business of the meeting. He demanded that our pay checks be increased from twenty-three to thirty dollars. "We're doing skilled work," Pat Ryan boomed in his challenging voice. "The minimum wage scale for journalists is a dollar an hour. Why should we work for less?"

Barnes glared at the union leaders with bloodshot eyes. He struck the desk with his fist. "You know what you can do with your demands!" he yelled. "More pay? For what? Misfits, bitches, bums calling themselves writers, just because the government is giving them a handout." He swept the papers off his desk, then slumped back into his chair.

With grim dignity, Pat Ryan and Paul Yellin opened the door. The others filed out after them. I stayed to pick up the papers and straighten the desk.

"Boondoggling bums!" Barnes passed his hand wearily over his forehead. "Christ! I might have been a poet, but instead I wind up director of a madhouse."

He started to get up and knocked over an ash tray. He waved his arms at the mess on the floor and began to ramble. "In my novel, death will be the hero—death—" With the voice and gestures of a John Barrymore, he declaimed:

"Life, like a dome of many-colored glass,
   Stains the white radiance of Eternity,
   Until Death tramples it to fragments.—Die,
   If thou wouldst be with that which thou dost seek!
   Follow where all is fled! . . ."

"Follow—where all is fled!" He lurched into his chair. "Listen. We're like the ghosts in *Outward Bound*. A ship of dead souls drifting in the dead of night. I know we're dead, but we keep on getting drunk, making love, and talking politics."

His eyes closed, and the crescents of dark skin below them stood out sharply. I looked from the overturned ash tray to Barnes sprawled in sodden sleep. I saw the beginning of the end.

━━━━━━━━━━━━━━━━━━━━━━━━━━━━━━━━━━

CHAPTER VII

SELLING NEW YORK TO THE WORLD

A FEW days after our disastrous meeting with Barnes, I opened the morning paper and saw on the front page the glaring headlines:

WPA OFFICIAL AND RED–HAIRED WRITER IN HOTEL FIRE

WRITERS' PROJECT DIRECTOR AND GIRL IN HOSPITAL

The tabloid story of a "drunken illicit tryst" was such a shock that I couldn't eat breakfast. W.P.A. was again under fire, lampooned as "counterfeit work, supported with taxpayers' good money." Impatient to find out what had happened, I hurried to the office.

The noise of the Writers' Hall rushed at me as I opened the door. A crowd was already there, piecing together the details. The scandal had blasted us all out of our ruts and made us realize the precariousness of our jobs.

Perched on his desk, Paul Yellin read to the avid listeners:

". . . John Barnes and Jean Williams admitted they had a few drinks in his apartment. . . . A bellboy, investigating the smell of smoke, discovered their bed in flames. . . ."

"Well, the fire cooked their goose," Paul said. He went on reading:

172

". . . The Project, which has been a source of trouble and embarrassment to the Administration, will be reorganized. It is reported that Colonel Somervell is determined to choose a director who will see that the *Guidebook,* upon which 600 writers have been employed for over a year, is promptly completed. The Colonel stated that the new director he will appoint will put less emphasis on sensationalism and more on efficiency and production. . . ."

We looked at one another in panic. The military threat of efficiency frightened us. Those of us whom Barnes had befriended knew we'd never get another director with his creative understanding.

Work was at a standstill. All over the huge hall there were knots of people, talking through clouds of smoke. The hum of speculation never ceased until the afternoon Somervell announced that Barnes had resigned and that Nathan Tashman was appointed acting director.

We waited for Tashman the next day, sitting at our desks like children awaiting the arrival of their new teacher. We already knew something about him. Our grapevine provided a complete *Who's Who.* We knew that he had published a mediocre novel years ago and that he had been a reader for movie companies and a writer of detective pulp.

Our first sight of him as he stepped out of the elevator filled us with alarm. His face resolute with purpose, he looked the picture of Somervell's idea of an executive. He was dressed in an Oxford-gray suit, white shirt, and maroon-striped tie. Our eyes followed his triumphant progress through the hall to his office.

All that day and for days after, the acting director was busy with reorganization. From his office issued memos, pink, yellow, blue, and white. People rushed back and forth with fear in their faces. Tashman's "new standard of production" drove us all into a panic of hurry and confusion. One by one, we were called before him. Although I was prepared for anything, I trembled as I walked in with my manuscript.

"There's no record here of any work you have done," he began.

"I am working on a novel. I have part of it here. . . ."

"Oh, yes, I know—the great American novel." The frown of authority hid the uncertain expression of his eyes. "I'm putting a stop to boondoggling."

"Mr. Barnes assigned me to the Creative Project. . . ."

"Mr. Barnes is no longer with us. I'm sorry, but we're cutting the Creative Project. The great urgency is to complete the *Guide*."

"But I'm not a journalist."

"You're free to write your novels after hours. No one is stopping you. But all of us on government pay must work for the government." He toyed with a new rubber stamp: "Acting Director." It was a powerful little stamp. I could feel his fingers itched to use it. "You haven't produced anything in years."

"Have you?"

"I'm a busy man." He arranged the papers on his desk. "I'd like to write novels, too, but I have a job. Washington has set a deadline for the *Guide*. We can only use writers who can turn in copy."

"I'd be glad to have you read my manuscript." I offered it to him but he waved it aside.

"My dear lady! This isn't helping the *Guide*." He looked at the clock with an expression of dismissal. "Report to Bailey hereafter."

A line of writers were ahead of me waiting for their assignments at Bailey's desk. Among them were Richard Wright and Jeremiah Kintzler. Wright looked amused, as if he were watching a circus, but Jeremiah clutched his brief case in bewildered horror.

"*Gevalt!*" he groaned in a whisper. "The world is coming to an end!"

Bailey, our newly appointed supervisor, called us to attention.

"I want you to know what's expected of you. Our job is to sell New York to the world. Our *Guide* is the biggest thing ever undertaken in this country. We have the biggest staff of journalists ever assembled under one roof."

Bailey went on like a Coney Island barker. "You must describe the great skyscrapers, theaters, office buildings, and churches that make New York the wonder city of America. You must play up the colorful sights, Greenwich Village, Harlem, the markets, the slums. Crowds of tourists from farms, mines, and logging camps will flock here to see the sights. The *Guide* will earn the thanks of hotels, department stores, and the movies for bringing crowds to their doors."

He picked up a paper and read the names of those who had failed to bring in the required wordage. "There's going to be a change," he threatened. "Those who can't produce will be fired and new ones hired. You artists think the government owes you a living. Well, it doesn't. Whether you live or not doesn't matter unless you give value for value received. Hereafter, the minimum for each and every one of you is two thousand words a day. Surely a paltry wordage of two thousand isn't much to do for your government in return for all you're getting."

"Wordage, poundage, yardage—" Jeremiah fumed. "Barnes was drunk only with liquor, but this faker is drunk with his own bilge." The old man tightened his hold on his brief case. "How could such a fool become a supervisor of writers?"

Bill Adams laughed. "He must have belonged to the right political clubs."

~~~~~~

CHAPTER VIII

WORDAGE MACHINE

MY NEW assignment was to catalogue the trees in Central Park. Most of us took the slips of paper that Bailey handed out like some bitter medicine we had to swallow. But Jeremiah Kintzler looked upon his assignment to write up the Fulton Street fish market as if he had been asked to break the tablets of the law. His *Life of Spinoza*, his reason for living, was rejected without even a reading.

"I'm the greatest living authority on Spinoza," he shouted. "Professors from Columbia come to learn Hebrew from me. And I, Jeremiah Kintzler, I am ordered to look up trivia for a guide to Babel! It's a desecration of everything holy!"

I admired the vitality of his rebellion, but, like the rest, I took the easiest way. I waited half an hour outside an office of the Park Department and got a list of the 253 varieties of trees in Central Park. The rest of the day I walked around the park and thought that doing wordage for Bailey wasn't so terrible after all. But the next day I was assigned to the library to look up the story of Hofmeister in Smith's *History of New York, 1779*.

The circulating department of the Forty-second Street library was a book traffic center as bewildering to me as a foreign country. S, Smith—I opened the first drawer of the catalogue, and then another. Smiths peopled the world. They crowded about me. Smiths who built colonies, wrote on finance and invented patent washing machines.

Down through endless rows of Smiths, my eyes blurred
—nowhere a Smith who had written *History of New
York, 1779*.

I took my place in line at the information desk.

"Where can I find Smith's *History of New York, 1779?*"
I asked the librarian.

"Look in the catalogue," came the voice of trained
efficiency, immersed in records.

"But I've looked under all the Smiths."

"Try New York."

I began hunting through the cards once more. Hundreds, thousands of cards with cryptic numbers and ab-
breviated descriptions. One of them must conceal the
information I sought. I began to feel a personal enmity
against these oblong slips of cardboard, a nervous irritation born of fatigue. This second search was as futile
as the first.

"I've looked through the entire catalogue," I told the
librarian. "I can't find Smith's *History of New York,
1779.*"

"Go to the Reference Room," she said. "Room 300."

Desperation did it. I found the card. I filled out a
slip. I handed it to the man. At last the book was in my
hand. Now for the story of Hofmeister.

But there was no index. I looked through the whole
book, page by page. There was no Hofmeister.

It was getting late. Lamps were being turned on at
every table and my assignment was still undone. The
whole day's work at those files gone to waste. I staggered
over to the central desk.

"I've looked all day for Hofmeister who lived in 1779."

The pretty face of a young librarian smiled up at me.
"Let's see." She turned to the catalogue. Inanimate index
cards came alive at her touch. She was like a trained
musician opening his piano. In a moment one book after
another, records, encyclopedias, yearbooks, were gotten
from the shelves and consulted.

"You must have the wrong name," she said. "We have

a record of William Havemeyer, but no Hofmeister."

The wrong name! It was almost evening and still no words for the wordage machine.

I was not putting the cards behind me. They would be waiting for me tomorrow and tomorrow.

The next morning when I signed the time sheet, Bailey demanded, "Where's your assignment?"

"I spent the day on a fool's errand. You told me to look for Hofmeister and there isn't any Hofmeister, only Havemeyer."

"Well, for Christ's sake! Why didn't you bring in the facts on Havemeyer?"

"But you asked for Hofmeister. How should I know that you don't know what you want?"

"After all, we expect you to use a little common sense." Bailey's voice was full of long-suffering patience. "I'm sorry, but we have a quota to maintain. Double word-age tomorrow."

When I met Jeremiah, going down in the elevator, his voice was a funeral wail. "*Nu?* Are you still cataloguing trees in Central Park?"

"Even Spinoza had to grind lenses for a living. You know he said in his hour of trial: 'Not to weep, not to laugh, not to condemn; but try to understand——' "

"Understand what? The robots who boss us? Either it's a Writers' Project or it isn't. Let's call it what it is. Organized madness."

He was interrupted by Richard Wright, who stopped for a moment on his way from the library. "Look! Did you see this?" He showed us the announcement of *Story Magazine* offering a prize of five hundred dollars for the best story by any writer on W.P.A.

"I've got plenty of stuff to send them," he said with refreshing eagerness.

"When do you find time to write?"

"At night. I'm going home now to work."

I watched him stride through the crowd—young, strong, immune to weariness. Whatever hardship he had known he had transformed into his creative drive.

Then I turned to Jeremiah and I saw the torment in his eyes. Both had a conscious goal that lifted them above the drifters that turned out the required quota for the *Guide*. Old Jeremiah fought himself into frustration, but every move young Wright made was headed toward fruition.

I didn't see Jeremiah for a few weeks. My assignments took me to Bronx Park to write up the zoo. When we met again at the timekeeper's desk, I was amazed at his rejuvenation.

He laughed with the high spirits of a young boy. "I have the great good fortune to be doing my own work again, the work that God Himself wanted me to do."

"So you're back on the Creative Project?"

He showed me the slip with his day's assignment: *"List the mayors of New York City."* But he laughed at it. He had learned at last how to outwit the martinets:

The morning Bailey had given him an assignment to the library, he felt like a dog seeing and smelling a bone, but held back by a tight leash. In the library were his beloved books on Spinoza, yet he was ordered to read historic junk for the *Guide*. He had dragged himself as far as the library, only to slump down at the entrance steps. He'd die rather than read stuff that didn't interest him.

As he sat there brooding, Bill Adams had stopped to greet him. When Jeremiah told him the cause of his despair, Bill slapped him on the back.

"Wake up and live! I've solved the W.P.A. problem: how to get by with the least possible work."

Bill said he had been assigned to catalogue the city museums. So he went to the tourist information service and there, in a couple of folders, he found all the dope he needed. He copied in an hour what was supposed to have taken a whole week to do.

"They've got all the stuff you need stacked up there in folders," Bill said. "So why waste time? The assignments we bring in go into the wastebasket anyway."

Jeremiah decided then he would play the game like the others. There was his nephew Benny, a boy with plenty of time after school, who knew the libraries. For a dollar Benny was glad to produce the required pound of flesh —the whole week's quota.

Jeremiah waved his cane triumphantly. "Now I'm so deep in my book it writes itself."

"Too bad the prize is only for fiction," I said. "You might have submitted your manuscript for the contest——"

"Contests, prizes are all vanity—temporal toys of children."

A cough shook his body, and left him so out of breath he couldn't speak, but his face still glowed with the smile of a man dedicated to his work.

"If you want to get rid of your cough, you must rent a better room." I reached over to straighten his tie. "For God's sake, it's about time you bought a new shirt with buttons."

"*Nu! Nu!*" he laughed. "When I'm dead, people will not remember the clothes I wore, or the room I lived in, but what I thought and felt. When they open my *Spinoza*, they'll lick their fingers from my words. Jeremiah Kintzler will be a name to remember."

But Jeremiah's joy did not last long. A few days later, he stood beside me as we signed the time sheet. His eyes were dark holes in his burned-out face. I had to pull his sleeve to get his attention. It needed two cups of coffee at the corner stand for me to find out what had happened.

He was bitter because his assignment had been changed. He had been told to write up the Street Cleaning Department. That his nephew could not do for him. So he struck.

He refused to do any more faking for the "required quota of words." He thrust at me the carbon copy of a letter he had sent to President Roosevelt.

"Read! Read only!" he urged. "I stayed up all night to write it."

I glanced at the first lines. "Strikes have been fought

for more pay, for fewer hours of work. *I strike for the right to do my own work—the work that no other man on earth can do but me. . . ."*

"What do you think of it? How do you like it?"

Before I could answer, he rushed on. "I count on you and every other writer who believes in honesty, in honor, to strike with me." He was shaking with emotion. "It was better—on relief— It's an insult to our intelligence! —copying catalogues, from catalogues, for catalogues!"

"You've forgotten what it was like on relief." I tried to reason with him. "I couldn't go back to the lonely hall room on the dole. With all that's wrong on W.P.A., it has brought us writers together."

"Together they crush the guts out of us. The quickest way to destroy people is to destroy their faith in their work. That is why they keep us so busy with wordage —to prevent those of us who once wrote from writing what we feel is true—to keep us even from thinking what we feel is true.

"Will you join me in my fight?" he implored. "All I want is what every artist wants—to give the world only that which comes out of his own heart."

What could I tell him? That you can't fight City Hall with an unpublished book on Spinoza?

He leaned against the railing of the Writers' Hall. Typewriters clicked memos in answer to memos, orders to change orders that had already been changed; copying paragraphs that had been copied from pages that had been copied from dust-covered books. Words dug up from dust to make more dust. Words to be filed away and buried in dusty cabinets till doomsday.

Jeremiah regarded the clattering juggernaut of efficiency with his sorrowful eyes. "Am I the only writer the wordage machine has not yet destroyed?"

He walked away, mumbling to himself, "I'll show them yet—here's one man who'll not sell his soul for a mess of politics."

~~~~~~

CHAPTER IX

PAYDAY

FRIDAY MORNING the six hundred of us stood in line, holding our identification cards, our names, and our numbers in our hands, waiting for our weekly checks.

The thought of our checks always charged payday with the excitement of a holiday. Those of us who had cigarettes gave away drags, those lucky enough to have any change left lent nickels for coffee.

We were a restless, pushing crowd, constantly breaking up into knots of shrill debate, but Mike Finley, the guard, was determined to keep us in a straight line.

"For Christ's sake! Let's have order here! Don't block the aisles!" He had caught some one edging up front. "All right, wise guy!" His eyes gleamed. "You people would get away with murder if I weren't around."

Payday was Mike's day of glory. He strode about, a uniform on short, thick legs, collecting our identification cards. But the anticipation of our money made us magnanimous; we could even laugh at Mike's roughneck tyranny.

"Don't push me!" Bill Adams scoffed, "I'm an American citizen!"

"I'll push anybody who blocks the passage." Mike jerked up his bullet head.

"Take it easy, Mike!" Pat Ryan gave the guard a friendly little shove. "You're not herding cattle."

"Jesus! Cattle would be easier to handle!" Mike wiped

the sweat from his beefy face. "It's my job to keep this howling mob in order. Hell'd break loose if I didn't watch you every minute."

He moved on, and as soon as his back was turned, the line sprawled out into friendly groups. Flirtations started, dates were made while propagandists expounded political views and union leaders attended to business.

A crowd had gathered at the bulletin board, reading an announcement of a special union meeting.

FIREWORKS!
YOU CAN'T AFFORD TO MISS THE
BIGGEST SHOWDOWN OF THE YEAR.
COME TO THE LOCAL. HEAR THE
GRIEVANCE COMMITTEE REPORT
ON VACATIONS WITH PAY ON WPA.

"Do you really think they'll give us vacations?" I asked.

"They will if we fight for it," Pat Ryan said militantly. "We have the same right to our vacations as other government employees." And he handed me a petition to sign.

One after another signed until it reached Miss Howard. She pushed away the petition. "I'll sign nothing of the kind."

We stared at the pale, white-haired lady, withered by the years into a straight line. And yet she stood against us all so erect, so conscious of her dignity, that she commanded attention.

Paul Yellin put his hand over her arm with the patience of a grownup reasoning with a child. "Haven't you worked hard all year? Couldn't you use a vacation in this sweltering heat?"

Miss Howard pulled her arm away. "I don't feel overworked."

Every one turned to look at her. It was the first time we had heard her speak with such open hostility.

"Some of us here—thank heaven—have a sense of duty. But you people, instead of being grateful for what the government is doing for you——"

"Grateful?" Yellin's mouth twisted into a wry smile. "Lady! They didn't hand us our jobs on a platter. We went out and shouted and fought for them. We made enough noise until they heard us in Washington."

"All this agitation is un-American."

"If we hadn't agitated, *you* would still be on relief."

"The trouble with you foreigners, you've been given privileges you haven't earned."

"Foreigners?" Pat Ryan laughed. "I was born here. Besides, this country belongs to those who inhabit it—not to those who inherit it."

We gathered around him, caught up in the energy that poured out of him as he talked. But Miss Howard stood there with her gaze fixed over our heads.

"My people have been here three hundred years. And you foreigners, who come here with nothing, do nothing but agitate."

Angry voices rose from every corner of the room.

"Your people were foreigners, three hundred years ago."

Bill Adams jumped upon the desk, clapped his hands for silence.

"Hear ye! Hear ye! Fellow-paupers!" he shouted, waving his hat up and down like a town crier's bell. "The question before us is not whether we came here with the Pilgrims on the *Mayflower,* or just got off the last boat, but how long will we continue to be here, without our checks? It's very simple. Are we going to starve or not? If I have to wait on this line much longer, you can carry me out on a stretcher."

Everybody laughed, except Miss Howard and Joe Lane, a wiry little man from Vermont who was standing beside her. With tightened lips she turned to him.

"Where are the real Americans? The decent, loyal, God-fearing Americans?"

Richard Wright closed the book he was reading and

shoved Ryan aside. "Why waste time with her? One signature more or less—what difference does it make?"

Everybody was so tense that Wright's common sense stood out like the strength in his young face. I marveled at the way he took part in everything happening on the Project and yet never became involved in the endless talk.

I asked him if he had any news of the story he had submitted to the *Story Magazine* contest.

"Oh, there are hundreds of manuscripts," he said, casually. "Nearly everybody on the Project is competing." But his words belied the anxiety in his eyes. He had the self-absorption of a great ambition.

The noon whistle sounded. It was time for lunch and we were hungry. A whoop of protest bellowed down the line.

"Damn it! Are they printing those checks? Where the hell is the paymaster?"

With the recklessness of a hungry mob, we forced our way into the director's office.

For the first time we saw the director afraid of us as we had often been afraid of him.

"I've been on the phone all morning, trying to locate the paymaster," he said. "I just found out he'll be held up till late this afternoon. There's nothing more I can do. You'll simply have to wait."

A groan went up the line and burst into a rebellious clamor.

"It's a conspiracy to humiliate us."

"The old tricks of reactionaries to wear us out waiting."

"Let's have a protest meeting right now," Paul Yellin called out. "Nominations for chairman!"

Everybody began to shout.

"Yellin!"

"Ryan!"

In this bedlam Jeremiah Kintzler sat alone in a corner, scribbling tensely on a margin of a newspaper. Back and forth, and over his head, the other writers shouted accusations, yelling for the paymaster, damning the politics and the red tape. But Jeremiah went on writing. He tore off the scribbled margins, opened his brief case and placed them tenderly inside an overstuffed envelope. He crossed to the window, stood there gazing out, lost in some thought that still eluded him. Then as he turned away again, he became aware of our eyes.

"God! Is there no end to this waiting?" He clawed at his throat with his bony fingers. "What work I could have done this morning, if I didn't have to come here to sign in for that miserable check!"

"Weren't you working all this time?"

"Who can work in this bedlam? If you put a canary in a room full of jazz, it dies in two or three hours."

He strode up to us, pointed to the clock with his cane. "Look at the time! You could build a pyramid with the hours wasted waiting here."

"After all, they're paying us for our time," Wright said, with a swift, flickering grin. "Twenty-three dollars and eighty-six cents is more than I ever earned writing."

Jeremiah didn't let him finish. "What do you know about time, you young fool? All you know is money."

Then he wheeled on me. "How can you smile like that? What makes you so happy in this madhouse?"

I could only look at him. Before, he had been frayed. Now he was in rags. His shirt was so torn that no safety pins could hold it together. He had been thin. Now the cheeks were dark hollows in the skull, but his eyes still burned with a relentless consecration to his dream.

He lifted his staff like a tattered prophet. "If all of you had had the courage to join me and write to Roosevelt——"

"What did you want us to do? Start a revolution?" Bill Adams demanded. "For you, nothing exists but the job of saving your soul with Spinoza. The rest of us have no souls to save—only our jobs."

"You think your jobs will be safe boot-licking your bosses?"

Jeremiah pointed to Bert Bailey a few desks away, sitting back, scanning the morning paper while a boy polished his shoes.

"Behold! The crowned king of *schnorrers* in his swivel chair!" Jeremiah scoffed. "Even a plumber must pass examinations before he can practice his trade, but any faker with a blue pencil can become a supervisor of writers overnight."

There was the bang of a chair falling. Bailey pounced into our group, glaring at Jeremiah.

"What are you griping about? Sore because you haven't done an honest day's work since you got on? You play sick when it comes to assignments, but you're well enough to come for your check. I'll not jeopardize my job shielding a chiseler like you."

Jeremiah's gaze fixed with the fascination of blind hate on Bailey's coarse face. Then he turned to the people around him.

"The wise man is never disturbed by the temporal authority of fools."

Bailey's neck went red. He pulled down his vest, jerked tighter the knot of his necktie. Without a word, he bounded over to his desk, took a typewritten sheet from the file, stamped it, affixed his signature, and handed it to Jeremiah.

"I was keeping this back because I was sorry for you. But now you've asked for it."

Jeremiah unfolded the note. It was pink paper. It meant dismissal. Although it was only a mimeographed form, Jeremiah read it aloud.

"You were previously notified that your work was *below the required standard.* You were warned that unless immediate improvement was made, further penalties would be imposed on you in conformity with W.P.A. regulations. Your work has continued to be *below the required standard.* You are hereby dismissed from the Project."

He tore the note with an air of indifference. But after

Bailey went back to his desk, Jeremiah crumpled the pieces, threw them on the floor, and stamped on them. He picked up his cane and brief case and strode into the director's office. I followed him.

Tashman was talking on the phone and did not notice our entrance. Jeremiah thumped with his cane. The director looked up and slammed down the receiver.

"Well? What's your complaint? Overworked? Breaking with the strain?"

"I am Jeremiah Kintzler. I know more about Spinoza than the greatest professors. I once occupied the editorial chair of——"

"Cut it short. What's your grouch?"

Jeremiah pointed to his brief case. "I am the author of——"

The director tapped with his pencil. "Once I also wrote a poem."

"Is it possible that a government rich enough to spend billions of dollars on W.P.A. is guilty of such poor management as to order a man of my intelligence to waste time cataloguing catalogues for the *Guide?*"

The director looked him over. Jeremiah returned the scrutiny, still confident.

"There should be a distinction between an author who has something to give and asks only to give it, and those to whom the Project is but a meal ticket."

Tashman glared. "You can either go back to your talmudic abstractions and starve, or do your assignments."

Jeremiah examined Tashman's white shirt front, the collar held neatly with a silver pin. Then he looked at the inkwell for a long, wild moment, but he only tightened his empty fist.

"You the head of the Writers' Project? You should be bossing a street cleaners' gang!"

Tashman kicked back his chair. "Get the hell out of here!"

The union meeting was in full swing on the line when Jeremiah came out. A delegation had been appointed to call on Somervell. The secretary read the resolution to be taken to the main office.

"Are there any more suggestions?" the chairman asked.

"I want justice!" came Jeremiah's hysterical cry.

Everybody turned to look at the skeleton in rags crying "Justice!" Here was innocence so pure it was close to madness.

"A resolution is on the floor," the chairman said. "If you have any grievances for the union to take up, wait your turn till we finish our business."

"That's the trouble with the union," Jeremiah denounced. "Always busy with business. Busy fighting for vacation, for toilet facilities. I'll give you something to fight for. Fight for a man like me who fights for the honor of all artists. I have been dismissed because I refuse to fake my work."

"All of us must do our assignments," the chairman said. "You're part of a group and you're acting like an individualist."

A long, slow look of pain came into Jeremiah's face.

"Aren't there enough time-wasters to keep up the show of busy work? I have *real work* to do."

Murmurs rose all around him.

"Who are you? Why are you any better than the rest of us?"

"You're sabotaging our jobs."

Jeremiah drew back with the dignity of a prophet dishonored by those he sought to save.

"I? I? Sabotage?"

"You're giving the enemies of W.P.A. ammunition," the chairman charged.

Jeremiah passed his hands over his forehead, his eyes fixed in space.

"There's a limit to faking!" The cry broke from his throat. "A limit to pretending it's a Writers' Project!"

The shrillness of his voice silenced every one in the room. It was the voice of chaos, doom, terrible as a curse.

"If I could only set fire to this place—blow it to hell! Blow up the sham, the hypocrisy!"

His shrieking stopped in a vomit of blood. His cane, his brief case clattered to the floor. He slumped, arms outstretched, blood flowing from his mouth. He gave a choking gasp, his hand went to his throat, and then relaxed.

There was a moment of horror. For the first time the hall was hushed in the waves of silence that rose from the body on the floor.

Bailey's telephone call for an ambulance broke the stillness. The crowd burst loose from the line, greedy for diversion. They pushed, they elbowed, impelled by a starved, almost hopeful, expectancy of tragedy.

When the doctor arrived, he bent over Jeremiah, applied the stethoscope, felt the wrist, lifted an eyelid.

"Dead!" he said, brushing the dust off his knees. The word passed from lip to lip in awed whispers.

"Bring the stretcher!" the doctor called.

A policeman, notebook in hand, led the way for the two stretcher-bearers. They carried Jeremiah out to the ambulance. A clanging of bells, and he was gone.

Released from the sight of death, everybody began to talk and move around. Jeremiah's brief case had been kicked under the desk. Just as I was picking it up, a door opened in the far end of the hall and the gray figure of the paymaster stalked in with the pay roll under his arm. Jubilant shouts greeted him. Immediately there was a stampede toward his desk.

With an expressionless face, he spread the yellow sheets of the pay roll, unlocked the black box containing the checks, and began calling our names.

Each person signed, and snatched his check with wolfish greed. One man lifted it to his lips. "Come to papa, darling," he crooned, and tucked it into his vest pocket.

"Don't spend it all on a Rolls Royce," the man next to him grinned.

"Nope! I'm keeping a dame in the Bronx with this."

"Me for hamburger and onions," said one of the clerks, making her way to the door.

No one noticed me as I carried Jeremiah's brief case out of the hall. I hurried through the streets, tense with excitement. I felt that Jeremiah had entrusted me with the fruit of his life—a manuscript that no eye but his had yet seen.

In my room I threw off hat and coat, impatient to open the brief case. But where was the manuscript he had talked about and for which he had fought and died? I hunted, and only papers of all sizes, clippings, scribbled envelopes, and bunches of notes, fell out. At the bottom was a mess of stuff, as if the trash from the wastebasket had been dumped there.

Jeremiah must have been contemptuous of order. He must have been too driven by the urgency of his thoughts to stop for the slowing discipline of organization. Time and great patience would be needed to sort all this.

The first notes I read were vague and confused, probably notes he had meant to throw away. I read on, but the more I read, the more disheartened I became with the stilted language.

"I have existed as Idea essence in God and my personality in God is a metaphysical entity, but in the body of time I'm a transitory nothingness."

Pages and pages of such barren abstractions. Every phrase creaked with the labor of incompetence. But I went on.

"Spinoza propels me with the speed of light out of my normality toward abnormal concepts of eternity, rips me out of the sockets of my emotional, passional life, and leaves me panting in a discorporate universe without star landing."

I paced the room, bewildered by what I had read. There must be a trace of the real Jeremiah somewhere. I tried to read again. But even when I came to the typewritten pages held together with dirty string, I could find only an occasional living passage. Out of the whole manuscript I picked a few paragraphs that touched me and I had to punctuate them to get their meaning.

"If I'm not for myself, who'll be for me? But if I'm for myself alone—who am I? There's the person I think I am, the person others think I am. But who is the real me? Who am I?"

And even this was not original. It came from a ghetto philosopher of the past.

Maybe there were other fragments buried in that jumble of notes, but I could not stand any more chaos. I stuffed the notes back into the brief case and hurried out of the house for air.

CHAPTER X

JEREMIAH'S *DYBBUK*

OUT IN the street, I felt as if I had left an unburied corpse in my room. I had to get rid of that brief case. Why had I grabbed it in the first place? Return it to the Project? It would only cause laughter. Another cruel joke on Jeremiah. I could not bear to have them laugh at him now that he was dead. What had he been to them? A clown who had exchanged a pushcart livelihood for a Mad Hatter's dream of authorship.

"That walking windbag!" Bert Bailey would rant at the sight of that brief case. "He's like all of you bums! Artists, my eye! Fakers! Frauds! Like all the rest of you, taking honest taxpayers' money for nothing."

It would have taken humility to know Jeremiah, and we had found a perverted release from our own frustration in egging him on to absurdity. To think of Bailey preaching honesty to us! Every one knew how he had gnawed and clawed his way to power. And we who were forced to keep up the bluff of "honest work" for him, shoveling meaningless words from one dead pile to another and then back again, were keeping up the colossal hoax that had snapped the last shred of Jeremiah's sanity.

Poor Jeremiah! His face had been a danger signal. The sight of him had sent people scurrying out of his way. I fled him, but it was no use.

The more I tried to shed the thought of him, the faster I walked, the more his ravings pursued me. "Why do

193

they call it a Writers' Project? Because we sign our names on the time sheet a dozen times a day? They watch us in the library and follow us up with the time sheet in the toilet. Stooges, gangsters spy on us. Are we citizens of free America or convicts in Siberia? All I ask is life, liberty, and the pursuit of happiness. It says so in the Constitution. If that's a lie, then whom can you believe? Where can you go for truth?"

I sought escape from Jeremiah's ghost in the brightly lighted Stewart's Cafeteria. Automatically I put food on the tray. I found a table and sat there, food untouched, remembering the way Jeremiah's torn shirt was held together with safety pins, the stubborn lock of hair standing up crazily to expose his baldness. The way he walked, head in air, swinging his cane, clutching his brief case, everything about him a caricature of genius.

Once he had walked me home from the library. He wanted my opinion of another letter of protest he was writing to the newspapers. But when he stood at my door, waiting for me to ask him in, I avoided his eyes and said I had a headache. I had been afraid if I showed him any sympathy, he might pull me into his futile turmoil.

That first day at the Project, I had smiled at his vanity when he showed me a yellowed newspaper clipping with his picture, taken fifty years before. In his own eyes Jeremiah had never grown older than that youth of twenty. He had died fighting for his faith in himself as a "young writer of promise."

"Hello! Hello, there!"

I looked up as from another world and realized I was in the noisy, crowded, smoke-filled cafeteria. Richard Wright was smiling down at me. I had never seen him so radiant.

"Great day!" he laughed, and drew up a chair beside me.

"There's a new shine in your eyes. Have you fallen in love?"

"In love with the whole world. I got me a riding tag clear across the Jordan."

He handed me a copy of *Story Magazine*. On the first page was his picture, with the announcement that the first prize of the W.P.A. Writers' Contest was awarded to Richard Wright.

"*Story Magazine* is proud that such a new and vigorous talent as that of Richard Wright should have won the contest. It is a tribute to the entire Federal Writers' Project that its assistance to the writers of this country should have enabled a talent such as Wright's to emerge into full growth."

"Five hundred bucks!" He held up the check for me to see. "And they're going to publish my book!"

In his eyes I saw my own elation thirty years ago when my first story was published.

"Congratulations! You had it coming to you!" I shook his hand. "Believe me. I know better than any one what this means to you. And if you're not too flushed with success to listen to an old lady——"

"Don't tell me nothing. Not now. You know, when I was a kid, they said I'd wind up on the gallows. I was no good, everybody said. My mother went to work and I ran wild, cutting school, stealing, lying, fighting everything in my way. I ran away from home and starved. I swept streets, dug ditches, but no matter what I did, or where I was, I always wanted to write. And, by God, I did it!"

It was in his face, the look of a man driving straight toward what he wanted. I knew the double-edged thrill of his triumph. It was not only recognition for his talent, but balm for all he had suffered as a Negro.

I thought of Hollywood when I had been as intoxicated with the triumph over my handicaps as Wright was now, wresting first prize from a white world. But he had the intelligence to take what he could get wherever he went and build with it. He would know how to take success for what it was worth and not become rattled by it as I had been.

He was smiling, blissfully aware of his achievement. And then a shadow of doubt effaced his smile.

"You want to know something? I'm scared to death. They asked to see my next manuscript. How do I know I'll be able to write anything as good as this?"

"That's just stage fright," I told him. "Don't try to do the next story until you've had a rest."

"But I don't want to rest, I can't afford to rest."

I looked at him and knew what he was in for. He had made his first step into the treadmill from which there's no respite. I knew his fear and haste to keep on producing—fear and haste more terrible than that of the day laborer who either starves or works himself to death.

And then I thought of Jeremiah and said, "The man who died on the pay line this morning was such a pure artist he lived it. He was so consumed by his vision of what he wanted to write, he couldn't come down to the sordid business of writing."

"That old guy! He was crazy, wasn't he?"

"There was a time when I thought so, too, but I'm beginning to wonder."

We walked out together. At the corner we parted. I watched him cross the street with his free, long-legged stride, head up, shoulders square. It was a walk of triumph, youth confident of power.

Did he know the source and substance of his power, the people who made him? He had climbed over their backs to reach the one opening of escape. Would his sudden opportunity only go to swell his ego? Or would he remember those he left behind? Would he use his chance to plead their cause? Or would he shake the dust of his past and succumb to ambition, the plague of those who rise from the poor?

His radiant face shamed my doubts. Time would catch up with him soon enough.

In one day I had seen the beginning of success and the end of failure. But the end is not yet, I thought as I turned home. I had to bury the corpse and wash my hands clean of the whole mess.

I walked up the stairs to my room and unlocked the door. On my table was Jeremiah's brief case spilling over with chaos. The despair of all aborted effort yawned out of that tattered, greasy bag. Writers whose stories had never found release in words, actors whose roles had never reached the stage, painters whose pictures had never materialized on canvas, lovers whose love had led only to loneliness. The passion, the ambition, the wasted lives!

Suddenly, roused from the nightmare of waste and loss, I picked up the brief case, carried it downstairs and emptied it into the ash can.

Like a sleepwalker, I returned to my room, gathered all my notes, my boxes of manuscripts, and carried them down to mingle my wasted years with Jeremiah's.

━━━━━━━━━━━━━━━━━━━━━━━━━━━━━━━━━━

CHAPTER XI

BREAD AND WINE
IN THE WILDERNESS

THE WRITERS' PROJECT became more desolate after Jeremiah's death. Every day it became harder to blind ourselves to the cold fact that we, like the privy-builders and road-makers of other public projects, were being paid not for what we did, but to put money into circulation. For right next to the supervisors who handed us our assignments were the desks of the new rewrite men who were actually turning out the *Guide*.

Newspapers clamored for the end of "boondoggling." And our director, frightened by the clamor, issued commands for more efficiency. The supervisors, with grim faces, counted the words, shortened the lunch hour and started a system of fines for lateness and other misbehavior. Every day there were new dismissals.

The time of signing in, which used to be the social hour of the day, was now the silent meeting of the condemned waiting for the ax of the executioner . . . the dismissal notice that would throw us back into the scrap heap of the unemployed.

Some of us were still too proud to sink back on relief, and we began job hunting. But the mere mention that we had been writers on W.P.A. discredited us for any honest work. It was necessary to make up a story to cover the time spent on W.P.A., and invent fictitious recommendations to get back to the honest, everyday working world.

And then suddenly, out of a clear sky, I found myself in possession of nearly eight hundred dollars. Zalmon Shlomoh, the fish peddler, had died and left me his lodge money and his phonograph with the cabinet of records. I had moved around so much that the letter from the "Sons of David Lodge" was weeks in coming.

Somehow this death money seemed stranger, more unbelievable, than the first ten thousand dollars from Hollywood. It was just like Zalmon Shlomoh to have paid his lodge dues with the pennies earned selling fish and send this gift to me after his death because I had fled him and his fish smells while he was alive. It was like one of the jokes he made as he wiped his gnarled hands on his sweater, gleaming with the scales of fish.

I saw again the odd twist of his back, and his eyes jesting with me at his own expense. "God sends always to the spinner his flax, to the drinker his wine, and to a Jew his wailing wall." With his Yiddish humor he hid his sorrow and squared himself with fate for his deformity.

Before depositing his check, I looked over his collection of records. Beethoven, Tchaikovsky, Caruso, *Eili, Eili, The Unfinished Symphony*. I played the *Moonlight Sonata*, the one he loved best. Once again, as I recalled the days on the East Side, I was possessed with the old longing to do something with my life before I died.

I wanted to write again with the honesty I knew when I lived on Hester Street. I wanted to make a new start away from the market place where I had lost myself in the stupid struggle for success.

At the public library I came across a pamphlet published by the state of New Hampshire, an open letter addressed to professional people with small incomes.

"Come to New Hampshire! Paint your pictures, compose your music, write your poems. Come, if you seek the peace and quiet of home. . . . A house and garden for the price of a hall bedroom in the city . . ."

There were pictures of white houses like jewels set

amid green hills and valleys. Among the famous homes
featured in the pamphlet was that of Marian Foster,
author of *Common Ground.* "Townsmen call her the un-
official first lady of New Hampshire," the pamphlet said.
"Her white farmhouse built by her great-grandfather is
a place where statesmen, scholars, and artists meet. The
world comes to her door."

Often when I had read Marian Foster's magazine stories
I had tried to imagine what she was like. Her peaceful
tales of small-town folk, *Friendship Village,* had opened
to me a new world where people were rooted in the hills
and valleys of the countryside around them . . . not
homeless, hunger-driven, like my ghetto dwellers.

It was the idea of being near her that drew me to Fair
Oaks. Because she was the opposite of everything I'd
known, I admired her. I thought that for the same reason
she would be interested in me and the people I wrote
about. I felt I could show her my work and ask her
advice.

One spring morning the sky was so blue, the air so
charged with hope, that I took the train to New Hampshire. I walked out of the tiny depot that afternoon with
the elation of a pioneer adventuring on new ground. The
place was not what I had expected from the neat pictures
in the pamphlet. Fair Oaks was a wide, wind-swept valley, the earth still brown, the trees just budding. In this
vast space a few farmhouses were scattered between
mountain roads. There was no main street, only a store,
a church, a school, and a gasoline station.

Marian Foster's house stood on a high hill overlook-
ing the village. All the way up the winding path to her
door, I was thinking how I would explain my coming out
of nowhere to ask her how I could go on with my life.

But when I saw her, she did not seem to think it
strange that I had come. People were always coming to
her with their problems.

Delight in the world glowed in her eyes. Her graying
ash-blond hair coiled on top of her head gave her face

a quaint femininity, a femininity which belied her tailored tweeds and energetic vitality.

I wanted to tell her my real purpose in coming to Fair Oaks. Instead, I showed her the pamphlet with the underlined words: *"A house and garden with a view of the hills for the price of a hall bedroom in the city."*

She looked at the pamphlet and then at me. Her gray eyes summed me up at a glance. She came to the point with the same directness that was in her stories. "How much rent do you pay?"

"Fourteen a month——"

"I know a house and garden you can get for twelve," she said, encouragingly. "Let me show it to you."

As we drove to the house, she turned to me. "No matter how small the amount you have to live on, many around you will be living on much less and enjoying life too."

We came through a garden into a sunny kitchen with an iron sink and a wood-burning stove. The house was empty, but there was a feeling of home about it. Then and there I decided to take it.

I went back to New York to dispose of my things. When I returned to Fair Oaks a month later, I was overwhelmed to find Marian Foster waiting for me at the station.

"How wonderful of you to take time from your work!" I told her.

"People are important," Marian said, helping me with my bundles.

I had expected to live for a week or two at a boarding-house until I could pick up enough furniture to start housekeeping, but Marian took me straight to the house. As we came through the kitchen door. I saw firewood piled by the stove. Instead of the cold emptiness of an uninhabited house, I found a kitchen ready to be lived in. The stove was lit, dishes were on the shelves, pots and pans in the cupboard.

"God on earth!" I cried. "Who did all this?"

"Your neighbors did it," she said. There was in her voice the elation of having accomplished what she set out to do.

She opened the icebox and showed me milk, eggs, and butter. In the breadbox there was a loaf of fresh home-made bread. Like a child on Christmas morning, I followed her into the living room. It was furnished, even with curtains and a rag rug.

I touched her arm. "How did it all get here?"

"Don't worry how it got here," she scolded. "Just enjoy it."

She went to the door. "I know you want to be left alone to unpack. Maybe you'd like to come for tea tomorrow."

I had always been afraid of the loneliness of the country, and here I was in a strange place, but already I had neighbors, and Marian Foster as a friend. I went to the window to see who my neighbors were, but the nearest house was a whole field away. Lawns, trees, and mountains in the distance were all I could see.

I sank into a wide-armed chair and looked about. This wasn't discarded furniture given like castoff clothes to the poor. Every piece was still warm with the touch of the people who had used it. They had given what they felt I needed out of their own homes.

Through the window as I sat there, I saw the golden light of sunset on the hills. For hundreds of years the homeless of Europe had dreamed of home. Home in America. And here at last I had found it. This was it. This gift of home.

On my walk along the mountain road to Marian Foster's house for tea the next day, I remembered Will Rogers upbraiding me for always harping on the past. "You've won success the hard way. Must you play the same tune forever? Suppose you give us another number." That's what I would do. I would learn from Marian Foster to be happy, learn to enjoy everything and everybody. Instead of the fear and anxiety with which I once wrote, I would write with joy and thanksgiving.

In my infatuation right after I arrived in Fair Oaks, I actually believed I could slough off my skin and with this new home begin a new life. The furniture that was presented to me, so steeped in the history of the village, would help me take on the life of the villagers.

"Have you everything you need?" Marian asked as tea was served.

I told her how much I had enjoyed my first lunch in the sunny kitchen.

"Only a city person could appreciate the flavor of fresh, creamy milk and fresh homemade bread——"

"We New Englanders could do with some of your enthusiasm." She laughed with pleasure.

I looked around her living room. The paneling, the brasses and pewters around the fireplace shone with the patina of age and years of polishing. The hand-woven rug, like the handmade furniture, the lamps, the pictures, reflected the peace of ordered lives. Was that the secret of Marian's self-assurance?

"Who baked that wonderful bread?" I asked as I rose to go.

"Mrs. Cobb, who lives in the house next to yours. She's a farmer's wife who writes poetry. . . ."

"Oh, a poet?"

"It may not be the kind of poetry you're used to. She couldn't talk about her poetry the way you New Yorkers would——"

"I'm crazy to know some one like that."

Marian looked at me. Her face did not show what she thought. "I'm afraid it will take you a long time to know these people." She paused and then went on. "If you approach them in the same quiet way they approach a stranger——"

"I don't feel like a stranger——"

"A personal relationship takes time," Marian went on. "It can't be pushed through as you push a button or turn a screw."

I was too excited that first day with my new home,

the country air, and the prospect of talking over my work with a writer like Marian Foster to listen to common sense.

On the way back, I saw Mr. and Mrs. Cobb at the window, eating supper.

"Hello!" I called. "Your bread was wonderful!"

She came to the door, wearing a faded cotton house dress. "I bake it every day," she said.

Mr. Cobb nodded to me from the kitchen table. He wore overalls, but even in their cheap, rough clothes, the Cobbs didn't look like farmers. He had the broad forehead, the lean, long features of the intellectual. Hard work and quiet patience were in her face.

"I hear you write poetry. You must show it to me some time——"

She smiled faintly. "You'll see it in the town paper."

"I don't want to bother you," I fumbled apologetically. "But I'm glad we'll be neighbors."

"Well, if there's anything we can do, do let us know," Mrs. Cobb said.

The next day when I went to the general store there were several men in wool jackets talking together in their drawling voices. One of them, a weather-beaten old farmer. was saying, "I turned over the south acre yesterday. I'm going to put oats in there." "Well," another one said, "I tried out that new seed last year, but——"

Their talk trailed off. They were sizing me up.

I walked up to the counter and asked for a box of oatmeal and a can of tomato soup.

"That'll be thirty-three cents," said the grocer, a tall gaunt man. "Seventeen for oatmeal, sixteen for soup."

"Oh!" I exclaimed. "In New York it's only fifteen for oatmeal and twelve for soup."

"This isn't New York," he said.

"Oh, it's all right," I apologized, putting the change in my purse. Their eyes were still on me as I walked out.

That evening as I ate my supper, I began to feel the fear that the country had always roused in me. Living a new life in a new place wasn't what I had thought it would be. It called for a self-confidence that I lacked. I had the old feeling of insecurity, trying so hard to please that I antagonized people.

In the city, for a nickel cup of coffee, or a ten-cent sandwich, I could walk into a cafeteria and see a continually changing current of faces. Some smiled and started talking to you at the counter, across the table. There was a fraternity of aloneness in the city. It was part of the common lot to be alone. But to be alone in a place like Fair Oaks was to be an outsider, a stranger, and separated you from the others.

The next few days I went around to thank the neighbors for their gifts.

"How could you part with that beautiful desk for some one you didn't know?" I asked the plumber's wife.

"When Marian wants anything," she said, "it's always for a good cause. We like to oblige her."

All my neighbors were hard-working women. If they weren't cooking or cleaning when I came in to see them, they were taking care of their vegetable gardens, feeding the chickens, or making their patchwork quilts.

One Sunday afternoon I took a walk past orchards of apples and plums, through a path of blackberry bushes, up stone steps to Mrs. Thompson's white cottage.

The men were on the lawn pitching horseshoes, enjoying a few hours of freedom from farm work. The smell of a New England boiled dinner, pork, cabbage, turnips and onions, came through the open door. Mrs. Thompson, a tall, angular woman in a blue dress and a flowered apron, was bent over a huge wash boiler, cutting soap. She stopped her work to draw up a chair for me.

"Sunday is the one day of rest the Lord gave us," she said, "but if I don't get a head start Sunday for Monday's washing, I could never get done all I have to do——"

"And with all you have to do, you've taken the trouble to send me that wonderful grape jelly!"

Her sun-browned face beamed. "You know what makes my jelly so good? I put a crab apple into my grapes. It makes a finer flavor and always jells."

Hard work and exposure to sun and wind had long ago dried the juices of youth from her cheeks. Her eyes, set deep in their sockets, were the color of the gray ledge in the back of the house.

"I hope you'll excuse the way I look." She pulled off her boots. "I've just come from looking after the chickens. Only half of them are left. Last week a weasel got into the coop and ate up some of our best hens. That cuts down on the eggs, and so I can't have any boughten things for the table."

Pushing a loose wisp of gray hair into the tight knot on top of her head, she went on. "We sure had some hard luck this year. The flood filled the meadow flats full of sand and dirt and ruined our cornfield, but cucumbers and tomatoes we have aplenty. Canning costs nothing but hard work. So I made a batch of piccalilli, sold it down to the store, and that was enough for taxes. There's always a way if you trust in the Lord."

I could only listen to her in silence. Her hardships seemed strange in this picturesque cottage with the hundred-year-old clock ticking reassuringly on the broad mantel, while outside in the distance the hills encircled the place in everlasting security.

I envied Mrs. Thompson her tangible woes, the fact that she could worry about chickens and a cornfield. If I could pin my troubles to something so concrete! I was plagued by doubts and uncertainties, the conflict between what I was and what I wanted to be, the consuming fear that I was nothing, nobody—and the inordinate craving for approval.

Everything that happened to Mrs. Thompson disciplined her faith that whom God loves He chastens. If one thing failed, she knew she could turn her hand to something else. She was anchored in the God of her fathers. But I had abandoned the God of my fathers and had not found my own. And because I was so lost without God, I had such deep need for people.

When I was at the post office one morning, waiting for the mail to be sorted, I heard a voice saying to the post-mistress, "I just can't make her out. She's a Jew. I knew that soon's she's spoke. I says to Jim, she's just another one of those writers come to write us up——"

"We're harder'n the rock that goes into our walls. We ain't got souls, she says—" another voice added.

"Well, but I don't call it a mark of brains or soul to go spooking through the hills all hours of the night."

Everywhere I seemed to see suspicion and distrust. Was it my own fear I saw reflected in their eyes?

Thanksgiving Day I want to see the high-school pageant celebrating the landing of the *Mayflower* Pilgrims. I thought it might help me catch the spirit of the village.

The pageant began with a scene of parting from relatives and friends, heartwrenching good-bys to England. As I watched I felt closer to the Pilgrims, who crossed the ocean in a frail boat, than to their descendants, who merely continued to live in the land made ready for them. The Pilgrims had been dissenters and immigrants like me.

At the final scene of the pageant Marian Foster walked in. She stood still until every eye was on her, waiting for her word. Then she began in her low, rich voice.

"Here we are, all of us together in a spirit of thanksgiving, re-enacting the events of our past."

She knew her audience and they knew her. She spoke to that crowd as if she were talking to each one personally.

"The Pilgrims who founded our country founded it on the Christian traditions of justice and mercy for all. They are not only our physical forefathers, but the spiritual fathers of all who come to our shores, the last comers as well as the first."

She made the familiar words sound new. Her voice was so resonant and had such dramatic control, I felt she might have been an actress as well as the guardian angel of the town.

She ended her speech with "This is our pride, this is the greatness of our country, that each newcomer is given a chance to contribute to the common good."

As we walked out of town hall, Mrs. Cobb turned to me. "Wasn't the pageant wonderful?"

"Well, it was interesting, but I don't see what's so wonderful about ancestor worship." And then I added mischievously, "They say there was only one man among the Pilgrims on the *Mayflower* who could sign his name."

"What does that have to do with it?"

"Of course, it must have taken courage to travel to an unknown country," I said, "but what courage does it take for the descendants to carry on here?" Under her steady gaze, I could feel indignation mounting and I struck out. "I'd like to challenge Marian's words 'Christian traditions of justice and mercy' and tell her what's going on in the world."

"Tell me, why did you come to the pageant?" I had never seen anger under such righteous control. "You come here where every one is minding his own business. Thanksgiving is a sacred day in our lives. We have a just pride in our past and we glory in our traditions. And you from the outside attack us and find fault with us, for doing the very thing that you Jews have been doing for the past six thousand years!"

As I looked at her I saw her anger turn to compassion. "I didn't mean to hurt you." Humility was in her eyes. "We must learn to forgive people what they are"—she paused—"even before we know what makes them what they are."

The words surged out of her heart to mine from a deeper source than ordinary language. We walked on in silence.

When we reached her house, she stopped and said, "I can't ask you in, because the extra man, who's helping us with the harvest, sleeps in the kitchen. But if you'll wait here a minute, I'd like to give you something for Thanksgiving."

A few minutes later she came out with a package and handed it to me. Without a word, she walked with me to my house. And still without speaking, we sat down on the log in front of my door. It was one of those rare Indian summer moonlight nights that charged the silence between us with a timeless quality.

Her hand went out to mine.

The river of sorrow that the exiled Jew carries in his heart suddenly threatened to engulf me at her touch, and I blurted, "Tonight I was intolerant—I who suffered from intolerance all my life."

Mrs. Cobb turned to me, her face showing the same warmth that I had seen only for her own.

"I understand," she said. "Our village is slow to take in a stranger. Perhaps you don't realize that you put up a wall around you that shuts people out."

"I do?" The idea shocked me. "I thought it was the village that shut me out. Even you. I wanted to talk to you so many times. I never knew how to approach you."

"I'm glad we met tonight," she said. "There were early mornings when I was on my way to the barn to milk the cows, and I'd see you coming down the hill—so early that you must have walked in the dark—and I wondered about you, but I didn't want to intrude."

"How hard it is for people ever to know each other!" I said.

"You expect too much," she laughed. "You go around looking for perfect understanding, don't you?"

I started to laugh too—the first, free, unself-conscious moment I had enjoyed since coming to Fair Oaks—laughing at myself.

"You see things so clearly. You help me——"

"And you've helped me," she said.

"How could I have helped you?"

"You remind me of all that I once wanted and renounced." She looked toward the hills in the distance, remembering. "When I was young, teaching school here, I thought I was a poet. I had published a few poems and editors had praised them. But I thought I could never try my talent here, in this little town. There wasn't any one with whom to talk about it. Who would understand?

"I had to fight my parents, my friends, and the man I loved. It took courage to go away. And who was I to be sure I was right? Just a teacher in a country grade school. But I had to try it. I had to find out that I was no genius, that love is more important to me than my poetry. And so I came back and got married."

The moonlight animated the lines in her face. I wondered if thirty years before, when she was an eager girl dreaming of poetry, that face had been as beautiful as it was now. Whatever trials she had known she had transformed into tranquillity.

"There were times when I felt half cheated because I know so little of the world outside," she said. "I've been sheltered from the things you know——"

"You know all there is to know about the world," I told her.

She smiled, took my hand and pressed it as she stood up to say good night. "It's taken me all these years to realize that the whole world for me is right here."

Back in my room I opened Mrs. Cobb's package. It was a loaf of fresh-baked bread and a bottle of dandelion wine. Whether it was the release of our talk or drinking that dandelion wine, I slept that night the sound sleep I had not known even as a child. When I woke, my first clear thought was: How could I have been fool enough to imagine just because Marian Foster was everything that I was not, and her writing had everything that mine lacked, that my need for her would rouse in her a responsive need for me, that our differences would be a creative stimulus to each other! Why did I always ask so much of other people, and so little of myself?

It was at Marian's dinner to celebrate the Pulitzer award for her novel, *Common Ground,* that I finally saw the futility of all my attempts to become a Fair Oaks villager.

That night Marian astonished me with her elegance. Her gold-brown velours dress reflected the glints of her ash-blond hair. It was the kind of dress that an artist would have chosen if he were painting her portrait; but she seemed unaware of her appearance. She moved as easily through the room as if she were still wearing her tweeds. As always, I tried to imagine what life must be to one having her ease, her self-assurance. I tried to smile with her smile, but the evil that I knew kept me from her happy innocence.

As from far away, I heard the conversation around me. Walter McCormick, Marian's publisher, a tall, red-haired Irishman with blue eyes, was talking to Marian and her husband.

" 'Indian Summer of a Forsyte' is Galsworthy at his best," said Mr. McCormick. "Old Jolyon breaking through the traditions of his generation and the generations before him to touch beauty before he died——"

"Yes, it's a haunting twilight piece," said Mr. Foster. "The solid, acquisitive, middle-class merchant realizing in the end that he can take nothing with him."

"Whenever I read Galsworthy, I remember his definition of art," Marian said brightly. " 'Art is the one form of human energy that really works for union and dissolves the barriers between man and man.' "

"I never heard that before," said Mr. McCormick. "It's splendid. I must remember it. By the way, that reminds me, last summer I saw a Little Theater production of *Loyalties*. It's surprising how up to date it still is."

Loyalties! The meaning of the word, the theme of the play, flashed through my mind—what happened to a Jew who tried to get into English society. What would Zalmon Shlomoh say if he could see me here? See to what use I had put his lodge money? I could almost hear his laughter as he regarded me with his sorrowful eyes: "Jew! Jew! Where are you pushing yourself?"

"I'm a Jew!" I blurted.

There was a sudden click of silence. A look of embarrassment closed their faces. After an interminable pause, Mr. McCormick turned to me. "I'm an Irishman, but I don't think it's important to announce it."

After that I neither saw nor heard anything. I got away as quickly as I could. Outside, the cool mountain air washed away my confusion. With a sudden sense of clarity I realized that the battle I thought I was waging against the world had been against myself, against the Jew in me. I remembered my job-hunting, immigrant days. How often when I had sought work in Christian offices had I been tempted to hide my Jewishness—for a job! It was like cutting off part of myself. That was why there was no wholeness, no honesty, in anything I did. That was why I always felt so guilty and so unjustly condemned—an outsider wherever I went.

When I got into the house I began to pack my things. In the midst of my packing, I stopped and wrote a letter to Marian Foster telling her that I was going back to New York.

Her answer came the following day.

I found your note on my desk when I came in from a long stolen day of joy on the mountain! (I should have been laboring at my desk with a thousand letters to do, not to speak of my own work, neglected for weeks, because of such demands from outside.) But my dear husband is going to Wisconsin University to give a series of lectures, and he wanted one last long tramp on our mountains before he left, so I dropped everything and went over to Stratton where we had a Moses-on-Pisgah day of it, with such a grandly spacious view so full of glorious color. I do hope you will soak the color and splendor of the dying year into your heart before you go back to New York.

Do you know that passage from Emerson—one of my favorites—I keep it on my desk: "When a man has got to a certain point of truth in his career, he becomes conscious forevermore that he must take himself for better, or for worse, as his portion: that what he can get out of his plot of ground by the sweat of his brow is his meat; and though the broad universe is full of good, not a particle can he add to himself but through the toil bestowed on this spot. . . . It looks to him indeed a little spot, a poor, barren possession, filled with thorns, and a lurking place for adders and apes and wolves. But cultivation will work wonders. It will enlarge to his eye as it is explored. That little nook will swell into a world of light and power and love!"

Isn't this finely Emersonian?

With every friendly good wish,

MARIAN FOSTER.

I reread the letter, stabbed by Marian's cold, clear statement of facts that I had been too muddled to face. She saw at a glance what I had struggled for and failed to achieve, the gap between what I was and what I tried to be—and she could sum it up in a few terse sentences. So "finely Emersonian"!

The last morning at Fair Oaks I woke to the sound of the milk truck going down the road to meet the freight train. I had finished packing the night before. The room, stripped of all of my belongings, looked just as I had seen it the day I moved in. My eyes turned from the rocker to the highboy, to the mirror framed in sea shells. Those prim New England things looked back at me as at an intruding stranger. They belonged. They spoke of stability, security, a homeplace for generations.

I took my bags out on the porch and stood there looking at the picturesque white houses of the valley. It had rained during the night and the freshly washed grass sparkled in the sun. Sunrise lit up the hillside with the last flaming colors of autumn. I watched a farmer ploughing the ground in a near-by field. The place was beautiful, but the sky wasn't my sky, the hills weren't my hills. It was a beauty that pushed me back into my homelessness. I thought of the azalea in its dark, southern soil, banked against the old brick walls in clouds of glorious color; but transplanted from its warm native ground to the cold, rocky New England hills, all its rich loveliness is spent in its struggle to survive as a pale, stunted dwarf.

Mrs. Cobb stepped out on the porch next door and waved. "I may be a few minutes late," she said. "But I put up a lunch for you, and I'll be over in time to take you to the station."

She arrived in an old truck and got out to help me with my bags. Her face was harsh and drawn in the morning light. She looked just as I had seen her the first time I met her, tight-lipped and tired from hard work.

"So you're going back to the city?" The quick little glance from the corner of her eyes, not at me, but in my direction, betrayed how deeply moved she was but embarrassed. Was she sorry to see me go? Was it possible that I had meant something to her?

At the station, waiting for the train, we looked at each other across the gulf of our different experiences. That searching look unlocked all that had seemed incommunicable between us. The trees, the rocks and hills of New Hampshire, and all the stubborn, unapproachable aloofness in the people of Fair Oaks—I began to understand. I wanted to thank her for turning on her light in my darkness.

"Well—" She started to say something, but the sudden thunder of the approaching train swept us up in the maelstrom of noise. We clasped hands without speaking.

~~~~~~

CHAPTER XII

RED RIBBON ON A WHITE HORSE

THE TRAIN from Fair Oaks carried me to an uncertain future, but Mrs. Cobb's farewell at the station had left me on the crest of courage. While I was living there, I hadn't realized how profoundly she had given me of herself, her imagination, her understanding. From the first she had accepted me for what I was, not for anything I had ever done. And so she rekindled in me the vital sense of myself that I had lost when I fled Hester Street. She was as close to me there in the coach as if I were having Sunday breakfast with her in her kitchen. In my lap was the lunch she had prepared—sandwiches, cake, and fruit in neat parcels of waxed paper—a reminder of the warmth and generosity of a prim New England farm woman, the poet of the town, whose greatest poem was herself.

There had always been something haunting in Mrs. Cobb's face. Something that made me feel I had known her somewhere, known her for a long time. And now, on the train, it came to me where I had seen that look before. That expression at once serene and wise had been on my father's face.

The likeness shocked me. The idea that there could be anything in common between this reticent New England farm woman and the uncompromising, Old World Jew seemed preposterous. And yet—I scanned their features in memory trying to see what made them alike. The same purity and trustfulness was in their faces. The same

215

"devotion to something afar from the sphere of our sorrow" looked out of their eyes.

A memory I had been pushing aside for years came back to me. It was just after *Bread Givers* was published. I felt I had justified myself in the book for having hardened my heart to go through life alone. I described how my sisters, who had married according to my father's will, spent themselves childbearing in poverty. I too had children. My children were the people I wrote about. I gave my children, born of loneliness, as much of my life as my married sisters did in bringing their children into the world.

The pride in the new book filled me with a longing to see my father. Because I had fought him and broken away from him as a child, I was drawn to him as an adult, now that I was achieving my own place in the world. I felt good, magnanimous. Instead of sending him the usual monthly check by mail, I wanted to give it to him as a token of peace and so forget the terrible fights that had driven me from home.

I found him in his room, bent over the table with his books, his prayer shawl and phylacteries. He closed the Bible and peered at me.

"What is it I hear? You wrote a book about me?" His voice and the sorrow in his eyes left me speechless. "How could you write about some one you don't know?"

"I know you," I mumbled.

"Woe to America!" he wailed. "Only in America could it happen—an ignorant thing like you—a writer! What do you know of life? Of history, philosophy? What do you know of the Bible, the foundation of all knowledge?"

He stood up, an ancient patriarch condemning unrighteousness. His black skullcap set off his white hair and beard. "If you only knew how deep is your ignorance——"

"What have you ever done with all your knowledge?" I demanded. "While you prayed and gloried in your Torah, your children were in the factory, slaving for bread."

His God-kindled face towered over me. "What? Should I have sold my religion? God is not for sale. God comes before my own flesh and blood."

The eyes under the deeply furrowed brow retained the purity of a child and the zeal of a man in love with God all the days of his life. As I looked at him, I was struck by the radiance that the evils of the world could not mar. I envied his inward peace as a homeless one envies the sight of home.

"My child!" His eyes sought mine, as if something in me had touched him. "It says in the Torah: He who separates himself from people buries himself in death. A woman alone, not a wife and not a mother, has no existence. No joy on earth, no hope of heaven.

"Look around you. Nothing in nature lives alone. The birds in the air, the fishes in the sea, even the worms under the stone need their own kind to fulfill themselves."

The uselessness of my visit! Each time I came to see him, he reminded me that I was unmarried and attacked me for my godlessness. His Old World preaching drained the joy out of my life. The more we tried to reach each other, the deeper grew the gulf between us.

"You're not human!" he went on. "Can the Ethiopian change his skin, or the leopard his spots? Neither can good come from your evil worship of Mammon. Woe! Woe! Your barren heart looks out from your eyes."

His words were salt on my wounds. In desperation, I picked up purse and gloves and turned toward the door.

"I see you're in a hurry, all ready to run away. Run! Where? For what? To get a higher place in the Tower of Babel? To make more money out of your ignorance?

"Poverty becomes a Jew like a red ribbon on a white horse. But you're no longer a Jew. You're a *meshumeides*, an apostate, an enemy of your own people. And even the Christians will hate you."

I fled from him in anger and resentment. But it was no use. I could never escape him. He was the conscience that condemned me. "Can fire and water be together?

Neither can truth be in the market place. Truth grows in silence, in stillness, in the secret place of the Most High—not in sounding brass and tinkling cymbals. . . ."

Now, all these years after his death, the ideas he tried to force on me revealed their meaning. Again and again at crucial turning points of my life, his words flared out of the darkness. "He who separates himself from people buries himself in death. . . . Can fire and water be together? Neither can godliness and the fleshpots of Mammon. . . . Poverty becomes a Jew. . . ." He didn't feel himself poor. Poverty had never starved him as it had me. Having nothing only drew him closer to God. Homelessness, hunger, exile—Jews had survived them for thousands of years. What was there to fear in a shabby coat? He walked the earth knowing that the "kingdom, the power, and the glory" were in his own heart; and no worldly prizes could swerve him from his chosen path.

But this single-mindedness, this immunity to the changes around him—this strength was also his limitation. He ignored the world I had to live in and compromise with. Centuries yawned between us.

It was Mrs. Cobb who brought me back to him. She was like a still pool in whose depth I caught a glimpse of the self from which I had been fleeing. With new-opened eyes I saw the poverty of spirit that had kept me barren till now, the fierce obsession of my will to lift my head up out of the squalor and anonymity of the poor.

Years ago, in Hollywood, Samuel Goldwyn said to me that to tell a good story, you must know the end before you begin it. And if you know the end, you can sum up the whole plot in a sentence. But I had always plunged into writing before I knew where it would take me. If a story was alive, it worked itself out as I wrote it. Even when I began this story, long before I went to Fair Oaks, I did not know how it would end—that is, the meaning of the end. I thought I was writing the downward career of a failure. Goldwyn would have summed it up in a phrase: "From an author in Hollywood to a pauper on W.P.A."

I wanted to unburden my shame for having failed. But on the train as I faced my disgrace, I saw that Hollywood was not my success, nor my present poverty and anonymity, failure. I saw that "success," "failure," "poverty," "riches," were price tags, money values of the market place which had mesmerized and sidetracked me for years.

For a long time I sat still, staring at the passing scenery through which the train was speeding, pondering the loneliness in each individual soul. The struggle of man, alone with the feeble resources of courage at his command, against a universe that cares nothing for his hopes and fears.

I remembered a dream I had had the night before. I was on a train just like this one. People were getting off at various stations, but I didn't know where to get off, my mind became a blank. As the conductor approached for the fare, I saw I had lost my purse and I cried out, "Oh, my God! I have no money and I don't know where I'm going!"

The anxiety that had hounded me from the day I was born was ready to pounce on me again. It had kept me on the run all my life. Even when I came to Fair Oaks I was running, but I couldn't escape it. The ghetto was with me wherever I went—the nothingness, the fear of my nothingness. Marian Foster had given me all that could be given a beggar—a house, chattels, milk, bread —while I resented her for withholding what she could not give, the understanding that I thought would make me secure. I had sought security in the mud and in the stars, sought it in the quick riches and glory of Hollywood and in the security wage of W.P.A. I sought it everywhere but in myself. Suddenly I felt like that shipwrecked sailor who had been picked up, dying of thirst, unaware that the current into which he had drifted was fresh water.

A warm wave of happiness welled up in me. Often before I had tried to be happy, but this happiness now came unbidden, unwilled, as though all the hells I had been through had opened a secret door. Why had I no premonition in the wandering years when I was hungering and thirsting for recognition, that this quiet joy, this sanctuary, was waiting for me after I had sunk back to anonymity? I did not have to go to far places, sweat for glory, strain for the smile from important people. All that I could ever be, the glimpses of truth I reached for everywhere, was in myself.

The power that makes grass grow, fruit ripen, and guides the bird in its flight is in us all. At any moment when man becomes aware of that inner power, he can rise above the accidents of fortune that rule his outward life, creating and recreating himself out of his defeats.

Yesterday I was a bungler, an idiot, a blind destroyer of myself, reaching for I knew not what and only pushing it from me in my ignorance. Today the knowledge of a thousand failures cannot keep me from this light born of my darkness, here, now.

AFTERWORD

BY LOUISE LEVITAS HENRIKSEN

"Poverty becomes a wise man like a red ribbon on a white horse" may have been a ghetto proverb, as my mother, Anzia Yezierska, had the publisher print on the flyleaf of her book. But I've always assumed she was the ghetto sage who invented it out of personal necessity, and of course invented a story to go with it: that her father told her this "proverb" when she was a child, that in her youth she rejected its message, and then, chastened by the experience of wealth and its loss, that she came to realize that her father was right. Probably he warned her repeatedly against succumbing to Mammon, and Anzia the writer naturally gave his words more punch.

Less than anyone I can think of could she be trusted to tell the unadorned truth. Being the child of such a story-telling mother meant that after about the age of 7 I had always to distinguish the real from her fictions, especially about people I knew very well. For instance, she might tell me a story about someone she didn't like—an "allrightnik" or "fat belly," about his meanness, selfishness, greed—and forever after, that cousin, aunt, friend, or storekeeper was indelibly colored for me with Anzia's dye, although her story might turn out to be apocryphal. She may even have believed her invented tale, for she trusted her vivid intuition more than her eyes and ears.

True, the habit of invention is well suited to a writer. But the way Anzia practiced it means that this book,

Red Ribbon on a White Horse, although it is subtitled
"My Story," should not simply be called an autobiography. For it contains as much fiction as fact. Rather, it
is Anzia's conception or interpretation of her life, much
refined by art.

In less than 200 pages she tells, and then takes apart,
her Horatio-Alger-like story: that after disembarking
in New York from the steerage of an immigrant ship
early in the century, she worked in a ghetto sweatshop,
pulled herself out of that hopeless dungeon to become
famous and even rich by writing about poor immigrants
like herself, reached Hollywood during its golden years,
the twenties, and, in fear of losing her soul as she saw
other writers doing, deliberately turned away from its
seduction. So she lost her grip on success, sank back to
anonymity and poverty, to a job on the WPA Writers
Project during the Great Depression, and in old age
found unexpected satisfaction, even joy, in cir-
cumstances most people would call failure.

These facts are mostly true. But they are really only a
distillation from which, looking back when she was
close to seventy, she strained out the in-betweens of her
life because they didn't suit her literary purpose—such
as a university education, two marriages, motherhood,
schoolteaching, and twenty years more (her old age) of
living and writing after this book was published.

By such omissions she melodramatized the extremes
of her life—for example, telling how in the white-tiled
private bathroom of her hotel suite in Hollywood she
turned on the bathtub faucets and let them run "for the
sheer joy of it" because in the ghetto tenement, where
she had lived before, there had been one iron sink with
one faucet for eight families. She has thus skipped over
and obliterated the twenty years it took her after leaving the ghetto to reach Hollywood.

But the inventions which she chose to add to the
spare essence of her life, I think, make this fictional autobiography more truth-revealing. Her best creations

are the most believable. For example, the begging letter
from an old Jew which (on pages 91–92 of this book)
Anzia found in her mail at the time she was uncomfortably immersed in movie luxury. "I read in the
[paper] how . . . Americans are weighing you in gold
for telling them how black you had it in Poland," the
old man writes. His experience of America has been
the opposite.

> I beg you for a ship ticket [back] to Poland where I
> can die and be buried with the honor Jews give to a
> man of learning. . . .

> Better to die there than to live here among the
> money-making fat bellies–worshippers of the Golden
> Calf. . . .

Begging but proud, taking for granted that because
they have the same heritage he has the right to ask and
she the obligation to give, he is a haunting reminder
that she has entered Mammon. Anzia invented him en-
tirely "out of a guilty conscience," she once confessed to
a friend. He was a stand-in for her dead father, who had
always condemned her "godless" success. Throughout
each turn in her life she confronted her father's critical
judgment, actual or remembered, as she fought fiercely
against the traditions he expounded: that daughters
must obey their fathers, that women were born to serve
men, a woman without a man had no meaningful existence on earth or hope of Heaven, and that the pursuit
of wealth instead of God was evil. At the moment of her
first worldly triumph, it was natural that her father's
ghost should come to haunt her.

Something of his rigid, uncompromising faith in his
own righteousness contributes also to the personality
of Jeremiah Kintzler, another of Anzia's fictional em-
bellishments of the truth. Kintzler, encountered here
on the WPA Writers Project, is a threadbare scholar,

whose life has been devoted to a biographical study of
Spinoza. Ragged, scorning ordinary comfort, a man
in love with learning for its own sake, he talks exul-
tantly about the great book he is writing on Spinoza,
a book which, Anzia discovers, existed only in his
conversation.

It so happened that one of the actual employees of the
Writers Project was a charming, Harvard-educated, al-
coholic bohemian, slight, bearded, unkempt, who regu-
larly enlivened bar-room conversations with accounts
of his continuing creation, an oral history of the world.
The history, which he seemed to carry with him
everywhere in a huge bundle, was in fact non-existent.
From this elfin Bostonian, descendant of one of
America's first families, Anzia shaped her Jeremiah.
He is the spirit of all would-be or aborted writers
"whose stories had never found release in words, actors
whose roles had never reached the stage, painters
whose pictures had never materialized on canvas."
There is even some of Anzia's wished-for idealism in
Jeremiah; he is the ascetic she often imagined she
might be, although her lust for recognition and success
had pulled her in the opposite direction.

She did not invent the character of John Morrow in
this book, but she disguised him here as an attorney, the
rescuer who gave her the opportunity to escape from
ghetto sweatshops by making her his secretary. In her
real life, she was never a secretary and he was the inter-
nationally known philosopher-psychologist-educator
John Dewey, whom she met for the first time when she
walked abruptly into his Columbia University office, un-
invited and unannounced. Having read about this great
man's active support of many "causes," she decided to get
his help for herself; she had been denied proper teaching
credentials by the New York City Board of Education because of her lack of discipline and grooming.

Dewey was extraordinarily understanding and gener-
ous; he was the Pygmalion who gave her the confidence

to become a writer—for which, he told her after reading
her early writing, she had far more talent than she had
for teaching. Although they knew each other for less
than a year, their intense encounter in that time transformed her life. He reappears in other godlike guises
throughout her writing.

So *Red Ribbon* is larded with many small and large
fictions and exaggerations—too many to point to inclu-
sively—because Anzia would invent whatever she
needed to make her point. Just as the subtitle of this
book does not testify to an autobiography, so the title
does not truly state its theme, except in a literal sense.
The title says, prosaically: money doesn't bring happiness; but Anzia had a more original point to make.

Her true theme, the idea for *Red Ribbon,* occurred to
her more than twenty years before she wrote it. In
1925, when she was a celebrated success, *Cosmopolitan*
magazine offered her a larger than usual fee to write
about her experience of sudden wealth, and she wrote
"This is What $10,000 Did to Me." It was an honest ac-
count of how she received a comparative fortune for her
first book ($10,000 in 1922 *was* a fantastic sum) and, al-
though offered many times more than that in Hollywood, was shocked to discover there "the fish market in
evening clothes."

She wrote also of her nostalgia for the days of poverty
when she was with the people she belonged to, the poor.
Now she was cut off from them by acquired but ineradic-
able differences. Being rich was lonely. She wrote several pages more about her disillusionment, a disturb-
ing, virtually un-American confession that success
wasn't satisfying, and even a hint that life could hold
more valuable rewards, but the magazine editor cut her
short for lack of space. The fee she received was as large
as promised, yet she felt blocked, cut off virtually in
mid-speech. This provocation germinated over the
years into *Red Ribbon on a White Horse.*

In 1950, when *Red Ribbon* was first published, Anzia

was living in a furnished room. She had long since lost most of her money. It had been eighteen years since her previous book—an extraordinary "silence" remarked on by all the critics, who heartily welcomed her back to literature. The truth was, she had been writing throughout the eighteen years and had been unable to sell any of her stories. After her overwhelming success in the 1920s, she had turned a sudden corner in the Depression 1930s into absolute failure. The editor who accepted *Red Ribbon* had rescued her from obscurity.

One reason he did so was that the noted poet W. H. Auden had read and admired the manuscript, and had generously agreed, at Anzia's request, to write an introduction. His name could help to sell more books than hers could. In his introductory remarks, well suited to the 1950s, Auden noted that America consumes its idols, that many first-book writers had been silenced by the American competitive pressure in art as well as commerce. He said that Anzia's story was about her effort to find real values as a substitute for the false-glitter prizes offered to her and other artists who won the competitions. He also pointed out that the immigrant experience (which he had himself known in emigrating to the United States) was becoming the spiritual experience of Everyman, for the "community of tradition is rapidly disappearing from the earth."

But Anzia did not recognize her book in Auden's analysis; in fact, his introduction made her angry because she thought it was "high-brow," thus distancing Auden from her plebian writing. She had hoped for a piece of his great poetry instead; and so she took the outrageous liberty of cutting his fifteen typed pages of "abstract Audenia" (her critique) down to about ten.

Another poet, a well-known American writer who also read and praised Anzia's manuscript but on principle refused the editor's request for a jacket blurb, wrote that the crux of the book was the conflict between the tyrannical patriarch and his rebellious daughter who, in her conviction of absolute right, clearly resembled him.

All three theses are certainly proved in this book: that money doesn't make you happy, that money values lead to bad art, and that freedom requires separating yourself from all tyrannies, even that of parental love. But to me Anzia's theme is more than the abovementioned three. Perhaps John Dewey was trying to teach it to her years earlier, before she was ready for it, when he told her (as John Morrow does in this book): "You don't have to become. You suffer from striving. You try to be. But you are, you are already."

During a large part of her eighteen years exile from publishing, Anzia had been writing, revising, and rewriting *Red Ribbon on a White Horse.* By the time of its publication, she knew what she wanted to say, and how to say it succinctly on the last pages of her book:

> The ghetto was with me wherever I went—the nothingness, the fear of my nothingness. . . .
> Why had I no premonition in the wandering years when I was hungering and thirsting for recognition that this quiet joy, this sanctuary, was waiting for me. . .? I did not have to go to far places, sweat for glory. . . . All that I could ever be, the glimpses of truth I reached for everywhere, was in myself.

That *Red Ribbon on a White Horse* was published in her old age after years of rejection was a triumph for Anzia, the vindication of her stubborn will, despite the world's indifference, to persist as an artist. Although the book was enthusiastically received by literary critics, who recognized that she had grown in artistry during the so-called silence, it did not reach many bookstores in 1950, and it was soon out of print.

Today it is more widely read and appreciated. The sharp change in our cultural climate during *Red Ribbon*'s hibernation from 1950 to the present is bound to affect a modern reader's response to Anzia's last book. This lonely woman's fight to live by her own standards, against her father's and her people's traditions, against authority's demand that she conform to custom as a wife, a mother, a schoolteacher, and even as a writer, seems courageous today. All the rules and edicts which she flouted by herself have come into question, and many have been overturned. Her fight for freedom is now recognizeed as heroic, not sinful. To this generation, my mother, who died in 1970 when she was close to ninety years old, is remarkably contemporary.